Timeless
Wire Weaving

THE COMPLETE COURSE

LISA BARTH

KALMBACH BOOKS

Kalmbach Books
21027 Crossroads Circle
Waukesha, Wisconsin 53186
www.Kalmbach.com/Books

Published in 2014
19 18 17 16 15   4 5 6 7 8

Manufactured in the United States of America

ISBN: 978-1-62700-076-5
EISBN: 978-1-62700-077-2

Editor: Karin Van Voorhees
Developmental Editor: Mary Wohlgemuth
Book Design: Kelly Katlaps
Photographer: James Forbes

Library of Congress Control Number: 2014944776

Contents

Introduction

Getting over the intimidation factor

When I was new to making wire jewelry, I admired many artists' work, feeling like a child with her nose pressed up against the glass. I was drawn in, amazed—and yet—intimidated by the beautiful complexity of the compositions. I puzzled over "how did they do that?" Now, when someone says they like my wirework but then quickly adds "I could never do that," it strikes a chord within me. The intimidation factor can be quite strong and difficult to overcome.

My main motivation for writing this book was to eliminate this intimidation factor. I want to bring wire weaving to everyone in a progression of project lessons that build upon each other, so that by the end of the course you've learned all that you need to complete the most advanced pieces, fearlessly. You'll begin with a simple woven earring, and each following design will add skills. By the time you have finished the book, you will have acquired many techniques to use in your own way as you create wire-woven jewelry.

WITH A FEW PIECES OF INEXPENSIVE WIRE, CREATE SOMETHING PRECIOUS.

It's only wire

Wire artistry never ceases to amaze me. How great is it that one can pick up a few pieces of inexpensive wire and create something beautiful and precious? If I make a mistake, I can seamlessly splice in another wire. Nobody will know, and I simply continue making the piece. There are a myriad of possibilities to enjoy. Unending variation is inherent in these weaving techniques. I feel as if I have just reached the tip of the iceberg of creative possibilities. That sure makes it exciting! Hand weaving is quite satisfying as you watch the pattern emerge from the wire as you work. You'll pick up a few pieces of wire and with a little practice, you'll create something beautiful and have a sense of accomplishment and satisfaction. Sure, it's only wire, but look at what you've done with it! The transformation is amazing.

Be the master of the wire

Wire tends to have a mind of its own. It is springy, it kinks, it knots, or it doesn't lie straight. Think of yourself as the "Master of the Wire." Don't let the wire take off in its own direction or kink up on you. Don't take no for an answer; get the wire in line! If you empower yourself to do the job with this strong attitude, you will find that half the battle is already won.

So, arm yourself with the strength of attitude to dash the intimidation of complex designs. Know that it is only wire — you can and will be the master of it. Let's begin the exciting journey of wire weaving together.

Lisa Barth

Getting Started

Wire Weaving Toolkit

The few tools required for wirework are easy to find. Most of what you need is available at your local bead and jewelry supply store. There are a plethora of options online as well. Although the tools are relatively inexpensive to purchase, you can create professional-grade artisan wire jewelry with them.

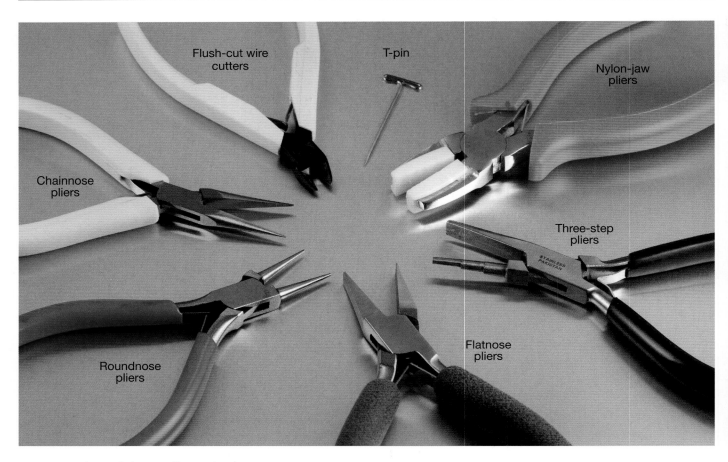

Flush-cut wire cutters
T-pin
Nylon-jaw pliers
Chainnose pliers
Three-step pliers
Roundnose pliers
Flatnose pliers

Here is a list of the well-stocked toolkit. You'll need these tools for all the projects in this book:

- Chainnose pliers
- Roundnose pliers
- Flush-cut wire cutters
- Flatnose pliers
- Three-step pliers
- Nylon-jaw pliers
- T-pins

If you are beginning in wirework, the three most important tools are basic pliers and wire cutters:

Chainnose pliers have flat, tapered ends and are used for stabilizing the wire while you are making a loop, or for turning the wire, bending it, or getting the wire in alignment.

Roundnose pliers have round, tapered ends, and are used for making loops and tight turns.

Flush-cut wire cutters have a flush-cut blade. If you look at the shape of the cutting blades, you'll see one side is angled and the other side is flat. The flat side is the flush side; it leaves a straight, clean cut. The angled side leaves a sharp, pointy end. You need to know which side you are using. Most of the time you want a flush-cut, so be aware of the tool's position as you cut.

As you advance in wireworking, you may want to invest in a few more useful tools.

Flatnose pliers have wide, flat edges and are ideal for straightening kinks or for making evenly spaced bends.

Three step pliers have three steps or levels on one jaw and a flattened jaw that holds the wire as you are using the tool. There are several reasons I like this tool. It makes it very easy to make consistently sized loops, simply by wrapping the wire around the same size step in the tool. It also gives me three good choices of loop size. And finally, the flat side that holds the wire doesn't create noticeable dents in the wire. When you pinch a wire with a round tool, such as roundnose pliers, it leaves small grooves in the surface of the wire. These marks can be irritating, to say the least, when you are trying to make a smooth, clean piece. A flat side will not do this and it is nice not to have to worry about all the little marks.

Nylon-jaw pliers have two flat sides that are coated with thick silicone. The sides are soft as they grip the wire and won't mar it. I use this tool mainly for straightening wire as it comes out of the package and for work-hardening, which means to harden up the wire a bit before use.

T-pins are very handy to have around. Use one to open up an area in a weave to fit another wire through. Do this by poking the tip of the pin where you want space and wriggling it back and forth. Sometimes the weaving wire needs to slide over a bit and you just can't get your tool in there to give it a push. A T-pin will get into the tiniest of spots so you can slide the weave any direction.

A **chasing hammer** flattens and strengthens wire. It has two sides: The flat side flattens out the wire, making a shiny surface, and the round side puts interesting divots on the surface. This

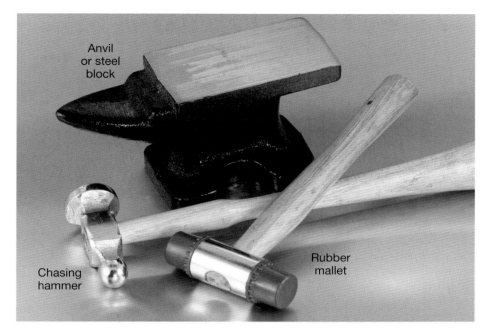

Anvil or steel block

Chasing hammer

Rubber mallet

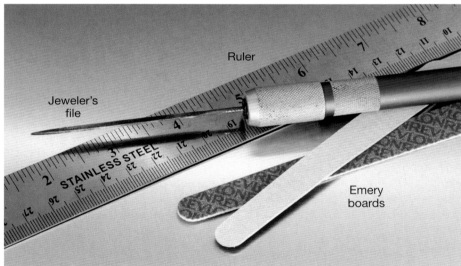

Ruler

Jeweler's file

Emery boards

texture can be very beautiful. Both sides work-harden the wire.

A **rubber mallet** also work-hardens wire. Its soft sides will not mark the wire or noticeably change the shape of the wire as you hammer the surface.

An **anvil** or **steel block** is a good surface to use with a chasing hammer or a rubber mallet. It comes in a variety of shapes and sizes. The small anvil you see here has a top surface that is 1¾x3-in. wide. It is quite small but does the job nicely.

Use a **jeweler's file** to file away any unwanted marks. Tiny, flat files are great for getting into small areas for "clean up."

Emery boards will also help remove unwanted marks on soft wire if you do not have a jeweler's file. They come in handy in a pinch.

A **ruler** is necessary for measuring consistent lengths.

Materials

Wire
Types

There are many types of wire. For just about any kind of metal you can think of (brass, steel, copper), there's a wire to choose.

copper wire

The projects in this book use copper wire from gauges 14–24. I chose copper because it is lovely on any skin tone and is easy to work with. It also oxidizes beautifully and creates a lovely patina as it ages. To me, copper only gets prettier with age as the patina deepens. Copper is also inexpensive, which makes it easier for you to relax while learning: You know it will not cost a lot to make mistakes, as it would if you were using sterling silver wire. Several variations of the projects are shown in sterling silver, but I always first do my projects in copper wire, and then go to sterling.

sterling silver wire

Sterling wire is very similar to copper in feel and is quite beautiful when woven. I like to give sterling wire a patina just as I do with copper. This gives it a wonderful aged look—that heirloom quality that I love.

Gauge

So what is the gauge all about? Gauge is a measurement of the diameter or cross section of the wire.

Have you ever looked at wire gauges and wondered why the numbers seem to go backwards? Why is 14-gauge wire thicker than 20-gauge? Logically, I would think the larger the number, the thicker the diameter of the wire would be, but in the American system of gauging wire, the opposite is true. In the history of making wire, the number of the gauge was based on how many times the wire had been stretched, or drawn, through consecutively smaller holes in steel plates to achieve a certain thinness.

So, a 20-gauge wire has been drawn 20 times and a 14-gauge wire has been drawn 14 times to reach its diameter. The 20-gauge wire is thinner than the 14-gauge.

Hardness

The hardness of the wire refers to the malleability of the wire, or how easy it is to bend. Wire comes in three different levels of hardness: full hard, half hard, and dead soft. When I was first learning, this was confusing to me because it did not seem necessary. After all, what does it matter? Well, after many years of wireworking, I see the advantages and disadvantages of the different types. Degrees of hardness for wire include:

full hard

This is very hard, fully tempered wire. It has very little malleability and is rarely used in jewelry making.

half hard

This wire is softer than hard but still has quite a bit of spring in it when shaped. This hardness of wire makes the wire stronger than soft wire but easier to manipulate than hard wire. It is good for earring wires, wire wraps, jump rings, and all kinds of connectors with wrapped loops. Half hard is quite tough on my hands when weaving, but I'm used to it. I usually keep quite a bit of half-hard wire on hand in several gauges.

dead soft

This hardness is the most pliable and the most easily manipulated. It bends very easily which makes it ideal for wire sculpting, spirals, and weaving. For beginners who are learning to weave, this hardness is the best. I have a very large stash of soft wire in many gauges on hand.

work-hardening

As you manipulate the metal wire by hammering, coiling, weaving, and bending, it will naturally stiffen, becoming harder to bend. This is called work-hardening. The molecular structure of the metal changes as you work with it; it becomes less pliable and even brittle if you push it too hard, and therefore, it can be more prone to breakage. You will soon see how weaving with wire will naturally harden the wire.

Focal stones and cabochons

I like to have a big stash of all kinds of stones from which to choose. Some of my favorite shapes are pear and oval cuts because they lend themselves so well to weaving the crisscross at the top. My preferred sizes are anything from 20–35mm because the weaving will make them appear larger as it frames the stones. For the projects in this book, I chose: two stone donuts (green jasper and blue quartz), two front-drilled flat beads, and two faceted cabochons.

Beads and chain

Choose copper beads with large (3mm) holes for bail beads. Copper spacers—such as a love knots and large-hole daisy spacers—are fun to use. A variety of turquoise beads are for embellishment, and a selection of copper chains come in handy as well.

Seed beads

Seed beads are inexpensive and add wonderful color and texture to any projects. I use 6º–15º seed beads. I love to add them to weaving projects. They are an easy way to mix things up a bit and personalize your jewelry.

IMPORTANT NOTES

Before you begin, it is important for you to know three helpful things:

1. Weave at the Ends of the Wires

Weaving is done on the right ends of the base wires and scooted along to the left as you weave by simply pulling each individual base wire out with your pliers, about an inch at a time. This is also how you center the weave, after you are done. Keeping your base wires short as you weave prevents tangling and helps you identify the order of the wires.

2. Avoid a Death Grip

Holding the base wires in a tight fist can bend them, preventing you from sliding them through the weave. Remember: These are the bones of the piece and bones are strongest when they are straight. Hold the base wires flat between your thumb and index finger, not with your fist.

3. Let the Wire Breathe

If your base wires cross as you are weaving, this usually means you are pulling too tightly on the weaving wire. You'll need to loosen up and only pull lightly; the wire needs to "breathe" a little so the base wires can slide through.

Terminology

These are the specific words I use that may be new to you to describe parts of the jewelry.

Bail Bead: Placed at the top of a pendant, the bail bead secures the bail wires.

Bail Wires: The top base wires, usually four of them, are used to make the bail. They extend through a bail bead and curve back around to form the loops from which the pendant is hung.

Base Wires: The horizontal weaving base is made from three or more 20-gauge round, soft wires. Think of the base wires as the project's bones.

Framing Wire: This is the outside base wire of a woven bracelet and is of a heavier gauge than the other base wires. It forms a strong frame.

Scrunching: This is the act of sliding the weave inward to condense it,

essentially making the weave more closely woven, so that it takes up less space on the base wires.

Spacer Bead: By placing seed beads as spacers on a base wire, you establish the spacing of the base wires as you weave. Without a spacer bead in place, it is hard to fit decorative beads into a weave later because the base wires will be too close together.

Splicing: Add a new weaving wire when the one you have has either broken off or is too short to finish the desired length of weave.

Stitch: The part of the weave that wraps two wires together to form the stair-step effect of the Flame Stitch is called a stitch. The bundles of two

wires at a time look like the stitches in bargello needlepoint.

Stretching: The opposite of scrunching, stretching is the act of spreading the weave out to take up more space on the base wires.

Turtlenecking: Also called giving the bead a turtleneck, this term refers to adding an accent bead on top of a weave. The bead is put in place with an add-on wire, which is then wrapped around the bead 2½ times to strengthen and protect the bead.

Weaving Wire: This 24-gauge, round, soft copper wire is the wire that creates the pattern on the base wires. Think of the weaving wire as ligaments that hold the bones together.

Working Clean: As you are working with tools, marks and little divots can mar the wire surface. Working clean means taking care to not put discernible marks on the wire from the tools.

Weaves

● Snake Weave

This weave is similar to braiding, with one wire coming up and over from one side and another wire coming up and over from the other. There are just three base wires and two independent weaving wires. Snake Weave can be used in multiple ways.

Single Snake Weave

1 Cut three 20-gauge base wires and a 24-gauge weaving wire to the length needed for your project. Using roundnose pliers, pinch the center of the weaving wire and pull each end of the wire to the opposite side of the pliers to make a small loop around the end of the pliers' jaws (**a**).

2 Pick up a base wire and slide the loop on the end so the loop sits about 1 in. from the end of the base wire. Place the remaining base wires on either side of this wire (**b**). The weaving wire should be beneath. I will be referring to this bundle of wires as base wire #1 on the bottom, base wire #2 in the center, and base wire #3 on the top. Support the three base wires with your index finger behind and your

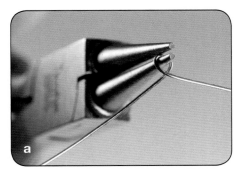

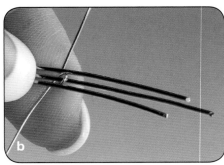

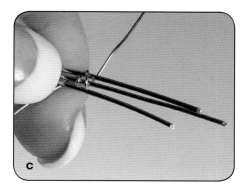

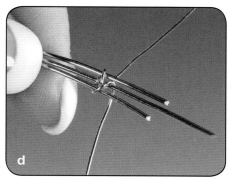

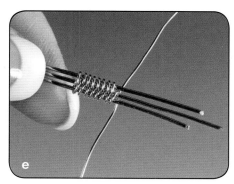

thumb on top (**c**). Try to keep them as straight as you can while you weave.

3 Bring the top weaving wire up and over base wire #3 and between base wires #1 and #2 very close to your thumb as it holds the wires. Bring the wire straight back, behind the bundle.

This places the proper bend at the proper place (**d**).

4 Bring the bottom weaving wire up and over the base wires to go between base wire #2 and #3. Bring the weaving wire straight down, making the bend behind the bundle.

Try not to pull too hard as you are weaving. The base wires should stay straight.

5 Repeat steps 3 and 4 to make the pattern (**e**).

Single Snake Weave with One Bead

1 Cut a piece of 24-gauge weaving wire to the length needed for your project. With roundnose pliers, pinch the wire in the center and pull the two wire ends in opposite directions to make a small loop at the tip of the pliers' jaws (**a**).

2 Cut three 20-gauge base wires. Pick up a base wire and string a seed bead of your choice on the wire

until it's about 1 in. from the end. Place base wire #1 on the right and base wire #3 on the left. Hold these three wires with your thumb and index finger. Slide the loop of the weaving wire on base wire #2, in front of the seed bead (**b**). Place the weaving wire ends underneath base wires #1 and #3.

3 Bring the top weaving wire up and over base wire #3 and between

base wires #1 and #2 very close to the first loop and seed bead. Bring the wire straight up, behind the bundle (**c**). This places the proper bend at the proper place.

4 Bring the bottom weaving wire up and over the base wires between base wire #2 and #3. Bring the weaving wire straight down, behind the bundle (**d**). This should be as close to the seed bead as possible, giving you the right place to make the bend.

5 String a seed bead on base wire #2 and slide it to the weave. Bring the top weaving wire over and between base wires #1 and #2. Bring the wire straight up in the back to make the bend (**e**). Keep the tension of the wire the same so your pattern will be consistent.

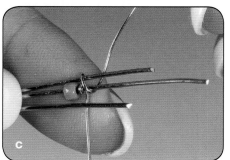

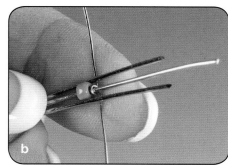

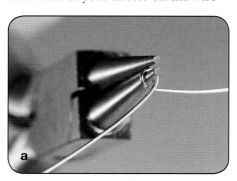

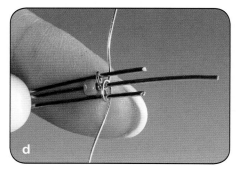

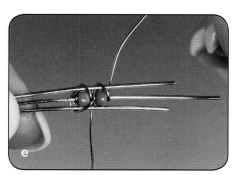

6 Bring the bottom weaving wire over the bundle and place it between base wires #2 and #3. Bring the weaving wire straight down to make the bend (**f**).

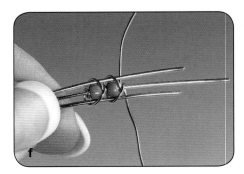

7 Repeat steps 3–6 to make the pattern of weave as long as your project requires (**g**).

Double Snake Weave

To achieve this pattern, double the wraps from the top weaving wire and then go the bottom weaving wire and do the same. Alternate the double wraps for the length of the weave you need for your project.

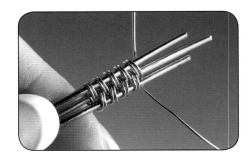

● Flame Stitch Weave

Flame stitch originated in the art of bargello needlepoint. Bargello consists of upright flat stitches that follow a mathematical pattern to create motifs. All stitches in the flame stitch are vertical, going over two or more threads, which is exactly what is done with the wire weave. In order to make the design a bit more easily understood, I have broken the pattern down into two steps: the uphill weave and the downhill weave.

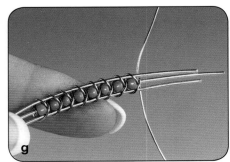

Here is an example of a flame-stitch motif. I took this picture when my husband and I were visiting Crathes Castle in Scotland. What a beautiful example of the Flame Stitch weave in the upholstery for this chair, which is hundreds of years old!

Uphill Wire Preparation, Single Wrap

Prepare the wires—before you start weaving, you must get the base wires ready and in place.

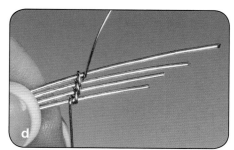

1 Cut the number of base wires needed for your project. There are five here, but the stitch is woven the same way with more or fewer wires. Cut the weaving wire to the length needed. Place the weaving wire on top of a base wire (#1), leaving a 1-in. tail. Wrap the weaving wire around the end of the base wire twice with nice, tight wraps. Leave the tail straight down and the rest of the wire straight up (a).

2 Place base wire #2 directly on top of base wire #1, with the weaving wire in front. Bring the weaving wire over and around the back to come between #1 and #2, making a single loop around #2. Leave the weaving wire straight up (b).

3 Place base wire #3 directly on top of base wire #2, with the weaving wire in front. Bring the weaving wire to the back and come up between base wires #2 and #3. Pull the weaving wire straight up for a single loop around base wire #3 (c).

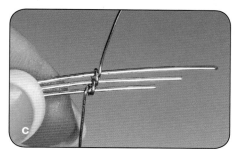

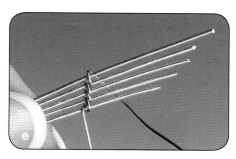

4 Place base wire #4 directly on top of base wire #3, with the weaving wire in front. Bring the weaving wire to the back and come up between base wires #3 and #4. Pull the weaving wire straight up (d). This makes a single loop around base wire #4, just as in step 3.

5 Place base wire #5 on base wire #4. Bring the weaving wire over the top and straight down the back (e). Stop, and you are ready to begin the next step of your project. You do not need to make a loop around base wire #5 because the act of bringing the weaving wire up and over it locks it in place and makes the weave consistent.

Downhill Wire Preparation, Single Wrap

Prepare the wires—before you start weaving, you must get the base wires ready and in place.

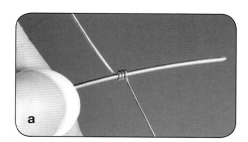

1 Cut the number and length of base wires and weaving wire required for your project. Pick up the first base wire (#5). While holding this wire close to the end, place the end of the weaving wire behind base wire #5, leaving a 1-in. tail. Wrap the weaving wire three times around and stop with the long end pointing down and the tail pointing straight up (a).

2 Pick up base wire #4 and place it directly below base wire #5 with the weaving wire behind it. Wrap the weaving wire around these two wires once and stop with the weaving wire pointing straight down (b).

3 Pick up base wire #3 and place it directly below base wire #4 with the weaving wire behind it. Bring the weaving wire straight up and between

base wires #5 and #4. Push the weaving wire up to the weave and make a bend straight down behind (c).

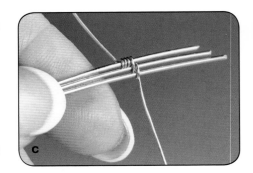

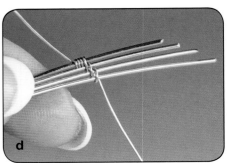

4 Pick up base wire #2 and place it directly below base wire #3, with the weaving wire behind it. Bring the weaving wire straight up and between base wires #3 and #4. Push the weaving wire up to the weave and make a bend straight down behind (d). Continue until you have added enough base wires for your project.

Uphill Wire Preparation, Double Wrap

To weave a double flame stitch pattern, you must get the base wires ready and in place.

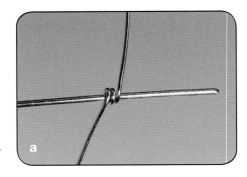

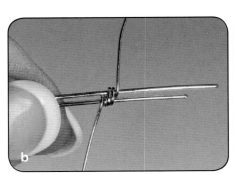

1 Cut the number of base wires needed for your project. Here, there are five bases wires starting with #1 on the bottom. Cut the weaving wire the appropriate length. Leave a 1-in. tail of weaving wire on the end and place it on top of the first base wire. Hold it with your left thumb and index finger as you wrap the long end twice around and stop with the long piece pointing straight up (a).

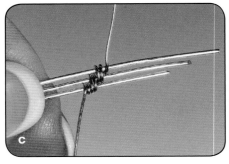

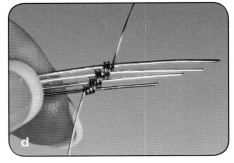

2 Pick up base wire #2 and place it directly on top of base wire #1 with the weaving wire in front. Wrap the weaving wire around both base wires #1 and #2 twice, bring the weaving wire between #1 and #2, and then bend the wire straight up (b).

3 Pick up base wire #3 and place it on top of base wire #2 with the weaving wire in front. Wrap twice around base wires #2 and #3. Come between #2 and #3 with the weaving wire and make a bend straight up (c).

4 Pick up base wire #4 and place it directly on top of base wire #3 with the weaving wire in front. Wrap both base wires #4 and #3 twice, come up

between with the weaving wire, and make a bend straight up (d).

5 Pick up base wire #5 and place it on top of base wire #4 with the weaving wire in front. Wrap twice around base wires #4 and #5, but do not come up between them (e). The five base wires are now prepared. If your project requires more than five base wires, come up between #4 and #5 and continue this pattern until you reach your last base wire.

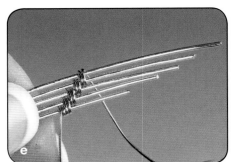

Downhill Wire Preparation, Double Wrap

Before you begin weaving, you must get the base wires in place and the weaving wire ready. Cut the appropriate number of base wires for your project (I am using eight—the outside or top base wire is 14-gauge and the following seven base wires are 20-gauge). Cut the weaving wire for your project.

1 Starting about ½ in. from the end of the 14-gauge wire, place the weaving wire on top, leave a 1 in. tail pointing down, and wrap it three times around the base wire. End with the long end straight down (**a**).

2 Pick up the next base wire and place it beneath the first base wire with the weaving wire behind it. With the weaving wire, wrap both base wires twice, stopping with the weaving wire straight down (**b**).

3 Pick up base wire #3 and place it directly beneath base wire #2 with the weaving wire behind it. Bring the weaving wire up, forward, and between base wires #1 and #2. Wrap base wire #2 and #3 twice. Stop with the weaving wire straight down (**c**).

4 Pick up base wire #4 and place it directly beneath base wire #3 with the weaving wire behind it. Bring the weaving wire forward and up between base wires #2 and #3. Wrap twice around #3 and #4. Stop with the weaving wire straight down (**d**).

5 Continue adding a base wire and wrapping twice around the last two wires twice until you have added the number of base wires required for your project. Here, I have prepared eight base wires, with base wire #8 pulled out a little farther than the others so it is easily recognizable (**e**).

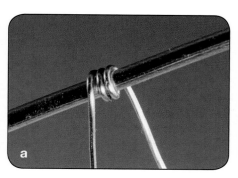

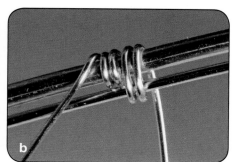

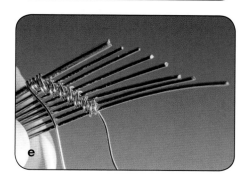

Downhill Flame Stitch Weave, Single Wrap

The pattern is down three wires, up two, and repeat until you are at the bottom of the hill.

1 Bring the weaving wire from the top base wire #5 straight down and behind. Count three wires from the top and come between base wires #2 and #3. Push the wire close to the weave. Make a deliberate bend straight up (**a**). Don't pull hard; make the bend at the right place and keep the bones straight and strong.

2 Go up two wires and come between base wire #4 and #5 right next to the weave. Gently pull the weaving wire straight down (**b**).

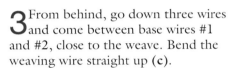

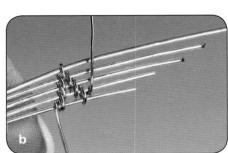

3 From behind, go down three wires and come between base wires #1 and #2, close to the weave. Bend the weaving wire straight up (**c**).

4 Go up three wires and go between base wires #4 and #5. Gently pull the weaving wire straight down in back (**d**). Stop here, because you are at the bottom of the hill.

Uphill Flame Stitch Weave, Single Wrap

The pattern for the uphill weave is up two wires, down one, and repeat until the top of the hill.

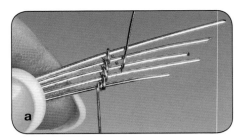

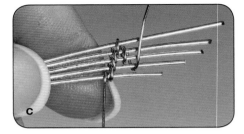

1 Start at the bottom of the hill. Bring the weaving wire around from the back and up for two wires, and go between base wires #2 and #3. Push the weaving wire close to the weave and make the bend straight down in the back by gently pulling the wire down (**a**).

2 Go down one base wire from the back and bring the weaving wire between base wires #1 and #2. Push the wire close to the weave. Bend the wire straight up in front (**b**).

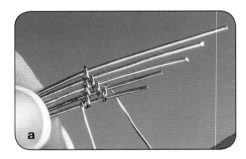

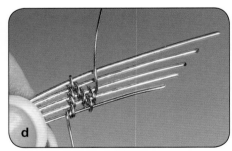

3 Go up two base wires and between base wires #3 and #4. Push the wire into the weave and pull down to make the bend in the back (**c**).

4 Go between base wires #2 and #3 and push the wire up to the weave. Bend the weaving wire up (**d**).

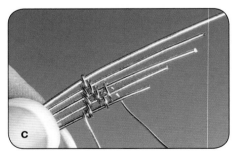

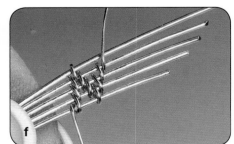

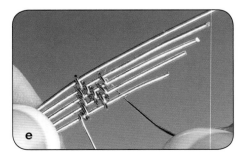

5 Bring the weaving wire up two wires to go between base wires #4 and #5. Push the wire up to the weave. Make a bend in the weaving wire by gently pulling down behind the weave (**e**).

6 Go down one wire from the back and between base wire #3 and #4. Push the wire up to the weave. Make a bend in the wire by gently pulling it straight up. You are at the top of the hill (**f**).

Uphill Flame Stitch Weave, Double Wrap

The pattern for the Uphill Flame Stitch, Double Wrap is similar to the Uphill Flame Stitch, Single Wrap. Wrap twice around the two bundled wires and then come up between them to make a half-step up. The pattern is up two wires, wrap those twice, and come down one wire to go between the two wires you just wrapped.

1 Starting from the downhill wire prep, bring the weaving wire up from behind, around base wire #1, and up two wires to go between base wires #2 and #3 and push the wire up to the weave. Head down and wrap base wires #1 and #2 twice. Bend the weaving wire so it is going straight down (**a**).

2 Go down one base wire to go between base wires #1 and #2. This makes a half-step up. Make a bend straight up in the weaving wire (**b**).

3 Going up two base wires, go between base wires #3 and #4 and then bend the wire down to wrap base wires #2 and #3 twice (**c**).

4 Go down one base wire to come between base wires #2 and #3, making a half-step up. Bend the weaving wire straight up (**d**).

5 Go up two base wires from there and go between base wires #4 and #5. Push the weaving wire up to the weave. Go down two base wires from behind and come up between base wires #2 and #3. Now go up and wrap base wires #3 and #4 twice (**e**).

6 Come from behind to go between base wires #3 and #4. Push the wire right up to the weave. Make a bend in the weaving wire so it goes straight up. This makes the half-step up in the weave (**f**).

7 Bring the weaving wire up and over base wire #5 and go around the back to come between base wires #3 and #4. Push the weaving wire up to the weave. Wrap base wires #4 and #5 twice (**g**). Do not come up between the two because you are at the top of the hill and you do not need to jump up a half step.

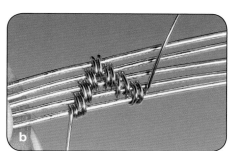

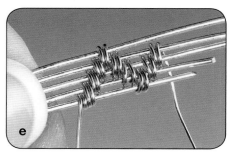

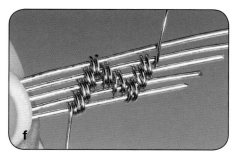

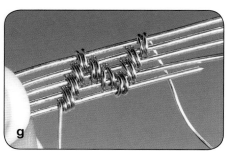

Downhill Flame Stitch Weave, Double Wrap

Starting from the Uphill Preparation weave, you are at base wire #5. The pattern is the same as the Single Flame Stitch, but with two wraps instead of one: The pattern is down three wires, up two, and wrap those two twice; repeat until the bottom of the hill.

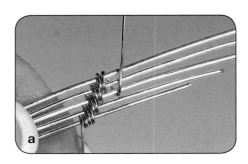

1 Go down three wires from the back of base wire #5 and come between base wires #2 and #3. Push the wire to the weave and make a bend straight up (a).

2 Go up two wires and go between base wires #4 and #5. Wrap base wires #3 and #4 twice, and bend the weaving wire straight down (b).

3 Bring the weaving wire from behind between base wires #1 and #2. Push the wire to the weave and bend it straight up. Go up two base wires and between #3 and #4,

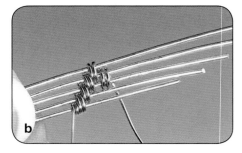

and head down to wrap base wires #2 and #3 twice. Bring the weaving wire around base wire #1 from the back to make the proper bend (c). You are at the bottom of the hill, ready to start uphill.

● Interconnecting Top and Bottom Weaves

When you weave with two independent weaving wires, you need to bring the work together so the two pieces become a single woven piece. The two middle base wires are shared as the center point.

1 Place the two woven sections so the last wrapped stitches on each side touch (a). There will be a gap between these wires because the weaving wires are doubled. Try to maintain the extra space as you make your next wraps.

2 Use the bottom weaving wire and wrap the shared wires twice (b). Here, with 16 base wires, the shared wires are base wires #8 and #9.

3 Continue with the bottom base wire. Drop down from behind and come in between base wires #6 and #7. Wrap them twice (c).

4 With the top weaving wire, go between base wires #8 and #9. Bring the wire up and wrap base wires #9 and #10 twice (d). Come in between them from the back and you

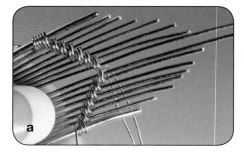

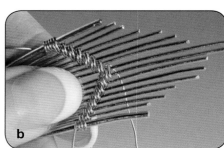

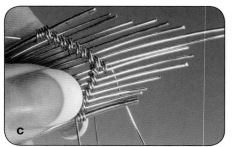

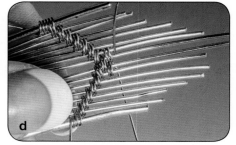

are ready to begin the next stitch. The center wires are stable and you can

continue weaving separately with the two weaving wires.

Techniques

● Turtlenecking

Turtlenecking is a decorative way of adding strength to a seed bead or other small bead that has been added on or placed on top of a woven section for accent. It is simply wrapping the bead two and a half times with a 24-gauge add-on wire. The technique adds a little copper shimmer on the sides of the bead. It almost looks like a small bezel and bolsters the bead with wire around its base.

1 On the back of the woven piece, at the intersection of the bottom and top weaves, there is one wire that is longer than the others in the pattern. Take a T-pin, poke it through, and wriggle it to open the wire (a). Do this to every intersection where you want to add a turtlenecked bead.

2 Cut a 24-gauge add-on wire the length needed for your project (about 3 in. per turtleneck). Thread the end of the add-on wire through the loop on the back opened with the T-pin (b). Wrap the end around the loop twice to secure. Cut the wire end close.

3 Bring the add-on wire through from the back between the two closest wires to the center, on the right. String a seed bead (c) and push it to the weave.

4 Bring the add-on wire between the two base wires closest to the center on the left. Pull the add-on wire tight from the back so it holds the bead upright (d).

5 From the back, direct the add-on wire through the same position you went through in step 3, right next to the bead (e) (see Tip).

6 Wrap the add-on wire 2½ times around the base of the bead. String the wire through the bead and pull tight (f).

7 On the back, bring the add-on wire through the second loop opened up with the T-pin. Go through the middle of the base wires and pull the add-on wire tight from the front (g). Now you are ready to add the next bead to turtleneck.

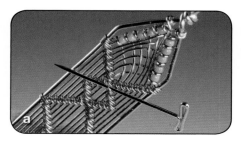

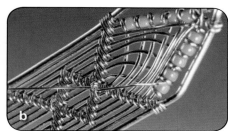

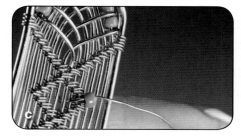

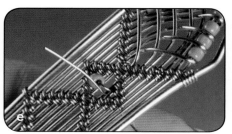

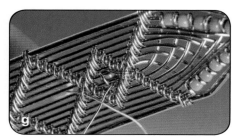

TIP As you pull the add-on wire tight from the back to the front, the wire will want to kink. Control this by putting your finger in the wire as you pull it tight to form a round loop. When you remove your finger, the wire has formed a smooth loop. If you do get a kink, stop before you pull it tight, pinch it straight with flatnose pliers, and carry on.

● Gooseneck Hook

A Gooseneck Hook makes a reliable connection and adds a bit of flair. I use this hook on bracelets and necklaces more often than any other connector. With 16-gauge wire, this hook adds about ¾ in. to the total length of your piece. 18-gauge wire makes a smaller hook that adds about ⅝ in.

1 Cut a 2¾-in. piece of 16-gauge wire or 2½ in. of 18-gauge wire. Make a small loop on the wire end with the tip of roundnose pliers (**a**).

2 Using flatnose pliers, grasp the loop to stabilize it and push the working end of the wire against the loop, beginning the coil (**b**). Shift the pliers to grasp this new part, and push the working wire around the coil again. Repeat until you have gone around the loop twice.

3 Using the tip of roundnose pliers, grasp the coil and make a bend (**c**). Continue pushing the wire around the coil halfway from the pliers.

4 Using the largest part of round-nose pliers, grasp the wire about ¼ in. from the coil, and push the end around the jaw (**d**).

5 Using chainnose pliers, make a tiny upward bend at the tip of the hook. Pinch the end flat (**e**).

6 Slide the hook onto the jewelry (**f**). A hook made from 16-gauge wire is strong without work-hardening. For 18-gauge wire, strike it a few times with a chasing hammer or rubber mallet on an anvil to add strength.

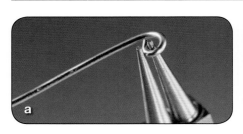

● Splicing

If your weaving wire breaks or you slightly miscalculate the length needed, you must add more wire without it being seen. It is easy to splice in a new weaving wire and nobody will ever know.

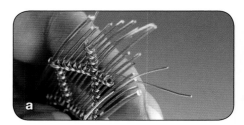

1 Cut a piece of 24-gauge wire long enough to finish. Bring the new weaving wire through the work to the front where the next step would begin had the wire not broken or run out. Leave a 1-in. tail in the back (**a**).

2 Hold the wire tail by pushing it next to the end of the original wire (**b**). Begin weaving just as you would if there had been no break.

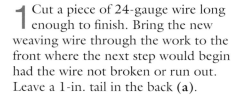
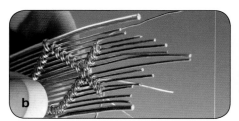

3 On the back, wrap the ends of the old and new wires around each other once. Trim closely (**c**). If one end sticks up, grasp it with chainnose pliers and bend the tip down. Pinch down to flatten out the splice and continue weaving as usual.

● Double-Wrapped Loop

A Double-Wrapped Loop is an essential wireworking skill: Make bails and links or connect dangles and chains with this technique. For a professional look, keep your loops consistent in size and orientation. Consider size in advance, and work on a wider or more narrow part of the roundnose pliers. Sometimes a small loop is appropriate, like in an earring. A large one may be needed for a bail. Place the loops consistently in the correct orientation. If the piece needs to lay flat, make the wrapped loops parallel. If the work needs the loops to turn 90 degrees, then make them perpendicular. One can always tell the overall quality of work by looking at the wrapped loops. To demonstrate, I will make a link of two double-wrapped loops with an 8° seed bead in the middle.

1 Cut a 3-in. piece of 20-gauge wire. With chainnose pliers, make a 90-degree bend in the wire about 1¼ in. from the end (**a**). Wrap the wire around the top of roundnose pliers so it makes a full circle.

2 Reposition the roundnose pliers so the loop is on the bottom jaw. Pull the wire to the right to form a 90-degree angle once again (**b**). Turn your wrist to the left slightly so the loop is centered.

3 Using chainnose pliers, stabilize the loop. With your fingers, wrap the wire tail around the wire stem twice (**c**). Try to keep the wraps tight against each other. This is the "double wrap."

4 Trim the tail with the flush side of the cutters (**d**) and pinch the end down.

5 String a bead on the wire and repeat the steps (**e**).

TIP for a dangle, string a bead on a headpin and make a Double-Wrapped Loop above the bead.

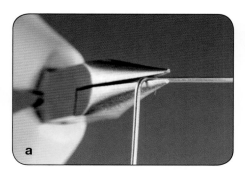

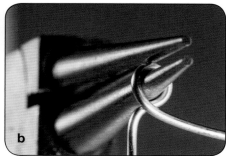

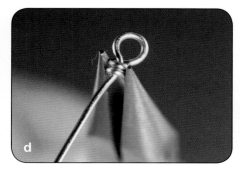

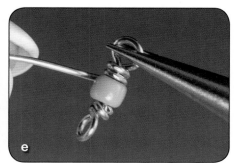

● Spirals

A Spiral is a large coil on an end of a wire. Spirals are a nice way of camouflaging an end and adding a bit of flair. They can be used in many ways.

1 With the tips of roundnose pliers, grasp the end of the wire and make a tiny loop (**a**).

2 With chainnose pliers, grasp the loop and hold it steady. Use your left index finger to push down on the end of the wire. The wire will start to coil. Let go of the loop, reposition the chainnose pliers to the left, and grasp the coil. Push down again to the left and watch the coil wrap around itself a little more (**b**).

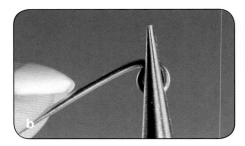

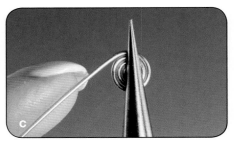

3 Keep pushing down to the left and repositioning the pliers on the right until the spiral is the desired size (**c**).

Spiral Earring Posts

This is a nice way of making an unusual earring post. If you have used spirals in the earring, it is wonderful to repeat the element in the post for a cohesive composition.

1 Cut two 4-in. pieces of 20-gauge wire. Using chainnose pliers, make a 90-degree bend in each wire ¾ in. from the end (**a**).

2 Pinch the wire right at the bend with the longer end above the pliers. Hold the smaller end tightly and begin to wrap the top wire around itself to make a coil (**b**). Try to keep the wire flat. If your wire has a mind of its own and pops up, or refuses to lay down, turn your pliers over and push down on the coil on a flat surface. That will teach it to make a flat spiral!

3 Wrap the coil 3½ times around. Using the end of chainnose pliers, make a space in the spiral (**c**). Bring the end of the wire around to the top of the earring post.

4 Place the earring on the wire so it rests in the space made in step 3. Hold the coil to stabilize it and bring the wire around to the top (**d**).

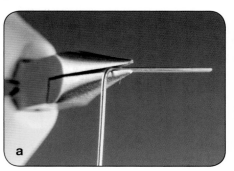

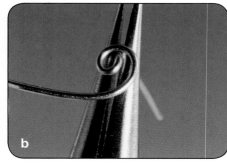

5 Turn the earring post around to work from the back. Keep holding the spiral to stabilize it and wrap the end of the wire around the earring post to make a tiny loop to hold it in place (**e**). Trim the end tightly and pinch it down. Trim the earring post to the length desired. File the wire end to make sure it is comfortable to wear.

Spiral Connectors

Connectors do just what the name says; they connect one piece to another. Making a Connector with the spiral in the center adds visual interest to your composition while also joining your pieces together.

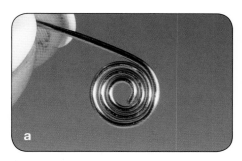

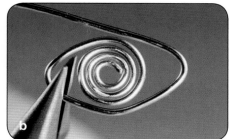

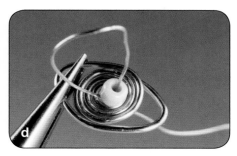

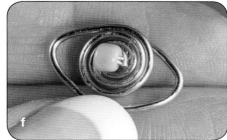

1 Cut a 5½-in. piece of 18-gauge wire. Make a spiral around the loop 3½ times (**a**).

2 Using chainnose pliers, make a space in the spiral on the left. Bring the wire around the edge to the right. Make another space (**b**). The shape resembles an eye. Try to get the spiral in the middle of the eye. Adjust the placement of the spiral by unrolling it a bit or tightening it up if it is not in the center.

3 Cut a 6-in. piece of 24-gauge wire. Wrap it three times around the end of the 18-gauge wire and trim it close. Bring the working end of the 24-gauge wire through the center of the eye from back to front. (This wire will hold a seed bead accent.) Make a small spiral 1½ times around the 18-gauge wire tail (**c**).

4 String a 6º seed bead on the 24-gauge wire and push it up to the spiral. Bring the wire through the center of the eye (**d**) and pull the wire tight from the back. Try to center the bead so it sits straight. It doesn't have to be perfect; you can adjust it when the wire has been tightened.

5 Wrap the 24-gauge wire under the top spiral twice to make a double coil. This will secure the wire and hold the bead in place (**e**). Trim the wire tightly and pinch down the end (**f**).

● Crisscrossed Finished Ends

For a tailored and clean finish, tuck in the ends of all those pesky wires with this method. This method tapers down a bracelet to make a loop for the clasp. This example has 16 base wires, but the technique can be easily adjusted to any number.

1 Center the weaving on the base wires. Find the two center wires. (Here, the two center wires are #8 and #9.) Pull base wire #8 to the left, over the top of the left side. Pull base wire #9 under base wire #8 and over the top of the right sides (**a**).

2 Using chainnose pliers, make a bend in the crossed wire #9 and direct it between base wire #1 and #2 (**b**). Repeat, directing base wire #8 between base wires #15 and #16.

3 Turn the piece over and work from the back. Trim the crossed wires to ⅜ in. and loop each wire around the outside 20-gauge base wire (**c**). (Here, the outside base wires are #2 and #15, next to the 14-gauge framing wires.)

4 String a 6º seed bead on each outside 20-gauge base wire (base wires #2 and #15). The beads give even spacing and add color. Repeat steps 1–3 and cross the next two wires in the center. Bend them to the back, trim, and loop them next to the bead on the outside 20-gauge base wires (**d**).

5 Continue to make a pyramid of beads and crossed wires (**e**). Trim and tighten each loop when it is in place. The outside 20-gauge wires should cross at the top.

6 Using flatnose pliers, bend in the outside framing wires to echo the angle of the bead pyramid. Cross them at the top, right over left (**f**).

7 Wrap the 20-gauge wires around the 14-gauge framing wires twice. Trim the end and pinch tightly (**g**).

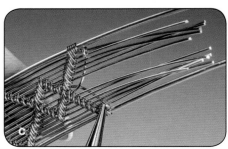

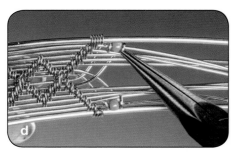

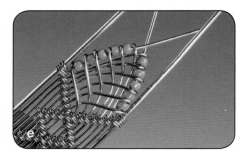

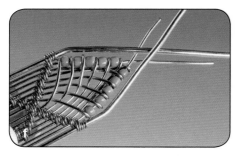

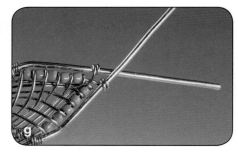

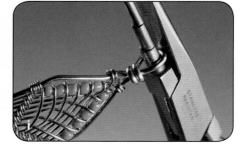

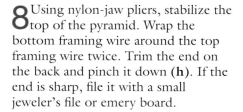

8 Using nylon-jaw pliers, stabilize the top of the pyramid. Wrap the bottom framing wire around the top framing wire twice. Trim the end on the back and pinch it down (**h**). If the end is sharp, file it with a small jeweler's file or emery board.

9 Trim the end of the top framing wire to ½ in. Using the largest step of three-step pliers, make a loop and tuck the end right up to the double wrap (**i**). Repeat on the other side.

● Creating a Finish With Liver of Sulfur

Liver of sulfur (LOS), potassium sulfide, is an oxidation agent used to place a patina on the surface of metal. Patina adds depth to the look of the weave that you have worked so hard on, giving an aged look and more contrast so we can see that gorgeous pattern. Use LOS on sterling silver, fine silver, or copper wire as long as it has not been treated with an anti-tarnish agent. LOS comes in several forms, including a solid form, that looks like chunks of chalky rocks, and a liquid form. The solid form is mixed with water and diluted. The liquid form can also be diluted with water or painted directly on the wire and rinsed off. Adding patina is a matter of personal preference. I like things that look like family heirlooms which have been around for years, loved, and passed down to the next generation.

Without LOS, the metal will naturally oxidize over time; I feel like I am just helping this wonderful process along so I can enjoy it sooner. If you are using sterling or fine silver wire, you may get an array of colors—greens and blues, golds and browns, and surprisingly, magentas. However, the color blending and rainbow effect are somewhat unpredictable. As soon as the metal touches the solution, the reaction starts and the reveal begins. I tell my students that liver of sulfur is "like a box of chocolates—you never know what you are going to get." Along with the surprise of different colors is the surprising rotten-egg-like odor that will hit you as you make the solution. Please don't let that intimidate you from using it; the smell is temporary. Using LOS really is fun and very effective.

LIVER OF SULFUR (LOS), POTASSIUM SULFIDE, IS AN OXIDATION AGENT USED TO PLACE A PATINA ON THE SURFACE OF THE METAL.

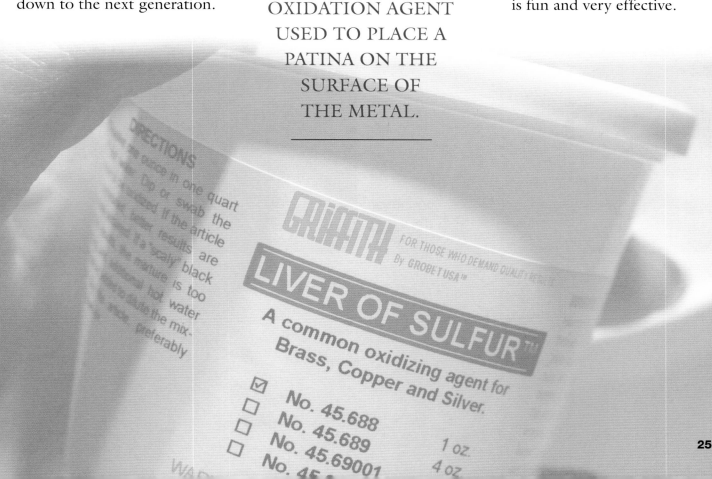

GRIFFITH

FOR THOSE WHO DEMAND QUALITY RESULT
By GROBET USA™

LIVER OF SULFUR™

A common oxidizing agent for Brass, Copper and Silver.

☑ No. 45.688
☐ No. 45.689
☐ No. 45.69001   1 oz.
☐ No. 45.   4 oz.

DIRECTIONS

Lump Liver of Sulfur

pea-sized lump of LOS
1 cup hot (not boiling) distilled water
1 cup cold water
1 teaspoon baking soda
2 plastic or glass bowls

Gel Liver of Sulfur

Dip a paint brush into it and whatever clings to it is enough
1 cup hot (not boiling) distilled water
1 cup cold water
1 teaspoon baking soda
2 plastic or glass bowls

1 Place your LOS in hot water and stir to dissolve. The water will change to a yellowish color. Both types of LOS work the same, but the gel form does not degrade in light and air the way the lump form can during storage. In the second bowl, pour a cup of cold water, add the baking soda, and stir until it is dissolved. Baking soda neutralizes and stops the development of the patina, preventing it from getting any darker or changing colors.

2 Dip the piece into the hot solution. I usually hold the jewelry piece with a piece of wire through the bail so I don't touch the liquid. Take it out quickly and see how deep the color is. If you like a bit darker, dip again until you get the depth of color you are happy with. Now dip the piece directly into the cold water solution. This will halt the action in its tracks. Dry it off with a paper towel. The copper wire will be a darker, toned-down version of its prior color and sterling or fine silver can take on many colors. Just keep dipping until you are happy with the result. On the left you can see a woven bezel pendant in copper wire that has not been dipped. On the left, it has been dipped so the color has mellowed. Liver of sulfur really changes the character of a piece.

3 Buff the surface with a jewelry buffing cloth. This will remove the dark patina from all the raised surfaces and make them shine. The more you buff, the lighter the copper or silver will become as the oxidation is removed. The patina stays in between the wires—all those wonderful little spaces created by the pattern of the woven design— and give that aged look, depth of texture, and makes your piece chock full of character.

Beginner Projects

Spiral
Woven
Hoops

This basic weave is embellished with colorful seed beads and woven into hoops with coordinating spiral earring posts.

Materials
• 3 ft. 20-gauge dead-soft copper wire
• 4 ft. 24-gauge dead-soft copper wire
• **2** 6mm round copper beads
• **46** 8º seed beads
• permanent marker (optional)

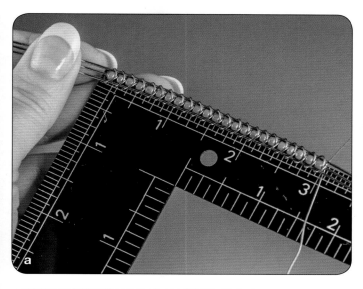

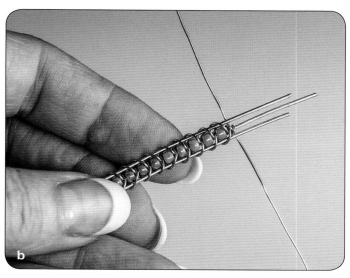

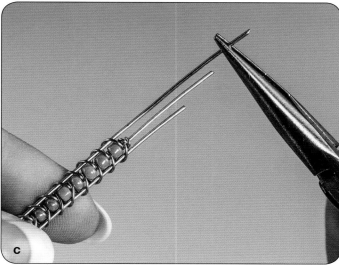

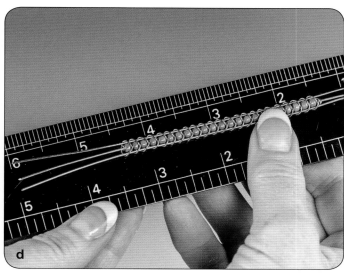

1 Cut three 6-in. pieces of 20-gauge wire for the base wires. Cut a 24-in. piece of 24-gauge wire for the weaving wire. Weave a 3-in. section of Single Snake Weave with One Bead (p. 11) (**a**).

2 Finish the weaving by wrapping each weaving wire once around base wire #2 (**b**). Trim close on the back.

3 Center the weave by grasping the end of each individual base wire and pulling outward with chainnose pliers (**c**). Slide the wire until there is 1½-in. of base wire showing on each end. If your base wires are not the same length, trim them so they are even. The size of your spirals are determined by how long these base wire ends are, so it is important that they are all the same length (**d**).

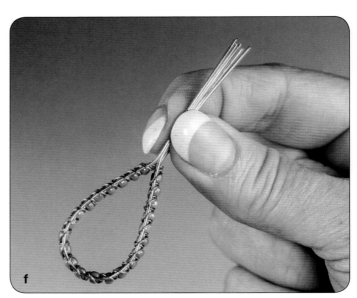

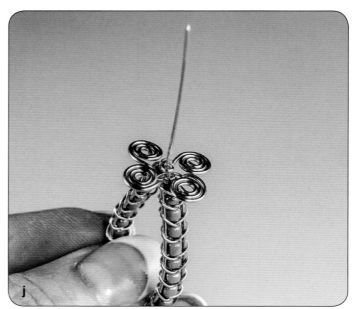

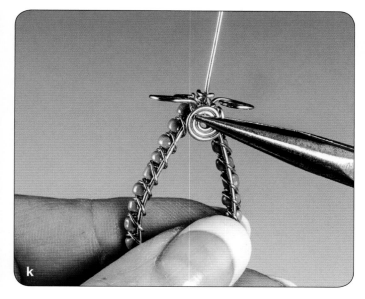

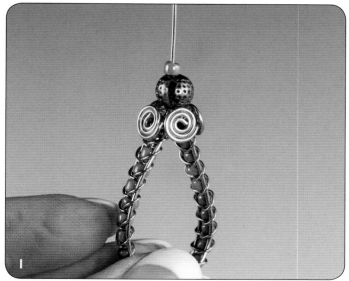

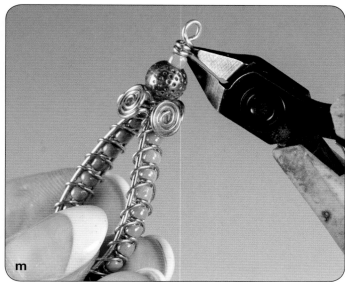

4 Bend the woven section to form a pear shape (**e**). The beginning of the weave will meet up with the end. Pinch all six of the base wires together with your thumb and index finger (**f**). I usually bend the weave around my thumb to get a nice, smooth shape for the bottom of the hoop. You also can use the barrel of a permanent marker as a form. Keep the base wires straight as they come together.

5 Bend base wires #1 and #3 straight out at a 90-degree angle from base wire #2. Do this on each side. Notice how the two wires are left standing in the middle, straight up. The weave remains in the same pear shape (**g**).

6 Using chainnose pliers, wrap one of the base wires that is standing up around the other. Make one wrap. It does not matter which one does the wrapping, as long as the wrap is tight and the stem wire for the bail is left straight (**h**). Trim the wrapped wire tightly against the stem wire, and pinch it down with chainnose pliers.

7 Make four Spirals going the same direction (**i**) (p. 22). The spirals should be about the same size, each perpendicular to the woven hoop, and on the same plane as each other (**j**).

8 Using chainnose pliers, bend each spiral straight down so that they make a little "box" around the top of the pear shape

(**k**). String a 6mm copper bead and a seed bead on the stem wire (**l**).

9 Make a small Double-Wrapped Loop (p. 21) at the top of the bail beads. Trim the end of the wrapped loop close (**m**), and pinch it down with chainnose pliers.

10 A spiral earring post is an option for the last detail of this project. Prepare a Spiral Earring Post (p. 22) and place the woven hoop on the post (**n**).

11 Make a second earring. Add patina with liver of sulfur (p. 25).

Donut
Bail
Pendant

Weave a bail for a donut-shaped stone (I am using a large 50mm jasper donut. The weave is adjustable to fit any size). Learn the Downhill Single Flame Stitch for the woven section, and learn how to embellish with seed beads for a dash of color and texture.

Materials
- 33 in. 20-gauge dead-soft copper wire
- 3½ ft. 24-gauge dead-soft copper wire
- 50mm gemstone donut
- 10mm large-hole copper bead
- 3mm bead
- **40** 8º seed beads
- daisy spacer with large hole

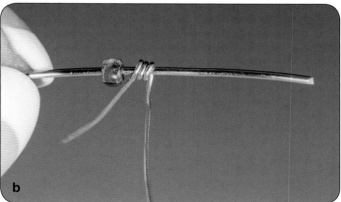

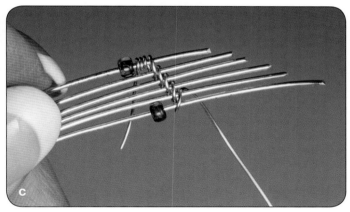

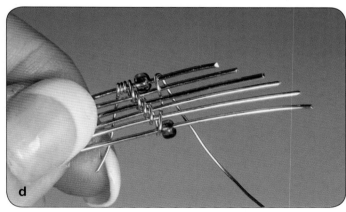

1 Cut six pieces of 20-gauge wire for the base wires. Cut one piece of 24-gauge wire for the weaving wire.

How much wire do you need for your base stone? Wrap a cord or string through the stone and mark the overlap (**a**). Measure this length. (My measurement was 2½ in.) Add 3 in. to that measurement for the length of the base wires. I cut six 5½ in. pieces of wire.

2 Pick up base wire #6 (at the top of the weave) and string a 6º seed bead about 1 in. from the end. This spacer bead makes room in the weave to add more beads later. Place the weaving wire to the right of the bead and on top of the base wire 1 in. from the end. Hold it with your left thumb and index finger. Wrap the weaving wire three times to the right of the bead (**b**).

3 Prepare the base wires for weaving by doing the Downhill Wire Preparation, Single Wrap (p. 13). On base wire #1, at the bottom of the weave, string a spacer seed bead, and then complete the last wrap of the Downhill Wire Preparation (**c**).

4 Remove the two spacer beads to the left and slide them back on base wires #1 and #6 to the right of the weave. Bring the weaving wire from behind up two base wires and go between base wires #4 and #5. This puts you at the top of the hill as you bring the weaving wire up, over, and straight down the back (**d**), making the jump behind the weave so you can repeat the downhill pattern.

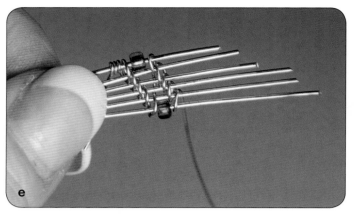

e

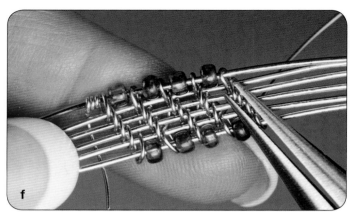

f

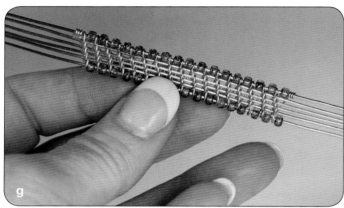

g

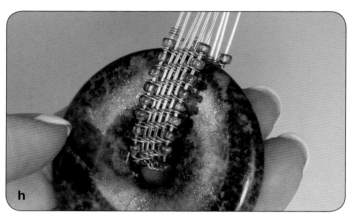

h

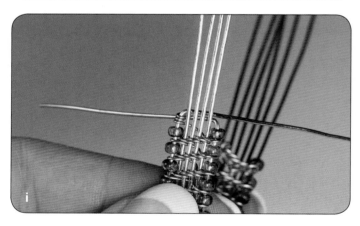

i

j

5 Begin Downhill Flame Stitch Weave Single Wrap (p. 16) **(e)**. At the bottom of every hill, at base wire #1, string a seed bead on base wires #1 and #6.

6 Continue with Downhill Flame Stitch Weave, stringing seed beads on base wires #1 and #6 as you go. If your stitches don't want to stay in neat, diagonal lines, pinch them with chainnose pliers to make them line up **(f)**.

7 Continue Downhill Flame Stitch Weave for the length you originally measured with the cord. When complete, slide each wire out individually until the weave is centered. Wrap the weaving wire three times around base wire #6 and trim the end tightly on the back **(g)**.

8 Push the weave into the hole of the stone and center the stone. Make a U-shaped bend to fit the stone **(h)**.

9 Remove the stone. There are several ends that need to be finished. Make a 90-degree bend inward with base wires #1 and #6. They will cross each other inside the weave **(i)**.

10 Bend base wires #2, #4, and #5 straight down on the inside of the weave, over the top of the two crossed wires. Trim all three wires to about ⅜ in. Using roundnose pliers, curl the ends of the three wires over the crossed wires to lock them in place **(j)**.

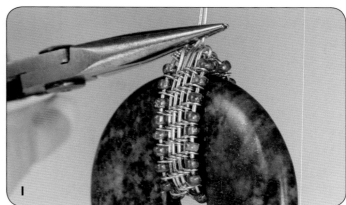

TIP *To make an embellished chain (o), make 16 Double-Wrapped Loops with coordinating beads (p. 21) and connect them directly to 16 pieces of decorative chain, about 1½-in. long. This is a nice accent for the composition. To finish, make a Gooseneck Hook (p. 20).*

11 Trim the two crossed wires close, up against base wires #2 and #5 (**k**).

12 Repeat steps 9–11 on the other side of the weave. Put the donut back in. With chainnose pliers, pinch the two #3 base wires that are standing straight up (**l**). This will bring the two sides in, right up against each other for the next step.

13 Make a double wrap around one of the #3 base wires. It doesn't matter which one, as long as it is tight. Trim the end and pinch it down (**m**).

14 On the remaining base wire, string a spacer bead, a 10mm copper bead, and a 3mm bead. Make a Double-Wrapped Loop (p. 21) at the top of these beads. If

you are adding a chain as pictured, connect the chain to the loop before you complete the wraps (**n**).

Woven Frame
Pendant

Ever have a beautiful stone with a hole drilled in the top that was screaming for a great setting? This project is your solution. A woven frame is just the ticket to show off a front-drilled stone and give a dash of personality. You can dangle anything in front: a charm, another stone, some chain—anything you want. I chose a twisted rope.

The weave is easy and elegant, and can be fitted to any size stone. Start with a simple shape to get used to fitting the weave to the contour of the stone, and then move to other shapes that challenge you.

Materials
- 27 in. 18-gauge dead-soft sterling-silver wire
- 6 ft. 24-gauge dead-soft sterling-silver wire
- 6 in. 26-gauge dead-soft sterling-silver wire
- 10mm bead with 3mm hole
- spacer bead with large hole
- dangle

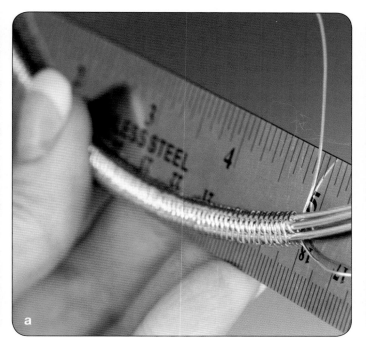

a

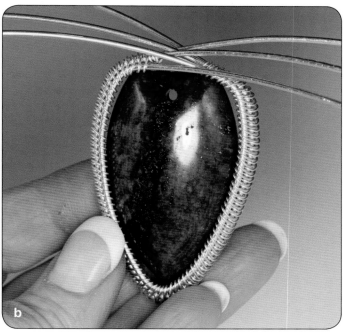

b

1 Cut three 9-in. pieces of 18-gauge wire for the base wires for the weave. If your stone differs from mine, measure the circumference using a cord or piece of string. Wrap this around the stone, mark the spot the cord crosses over itself, and measure the length. Add 4 in. The sum is the total length for each base wire.

2 Weave a section of Single Snake Weave (p. 10) equal in length to the circumference of your stone (a). Weave at the ends of the base wires and slide the weaving along as you go.

3 Mold the weave to the stone: Start in the middle of the weave, at the bottom of the stone, and go up from there. Push the weave against the stone and let the stone do most of the work to get the right shape. Crisscross the six base wires at the top, alternating left, right, and so on as if you were crossing your hands and interlocking your fingers (b).

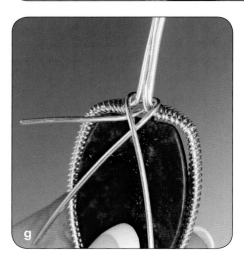

4 Bend the two middle base wires straight up and pinch them together to bring the two sides together (**c**). These two wires will become part of the bail.

5 Turn the piece over and work from the back. Bend each end of the #3 base wire straight back (**d**).

6 Guide the left #3 base wire through the hole of the stone from the back to the front (**e**).

7 String the dangle on this wire. Bring this wire under the crossed wires and pull it tight to the back (**f**).

8 Working on the back, bend the #3 base wire on the right straight up. It will become part of the bail. There should be three wires standing straight up for the bail (**g**).

TIP If the hole in your bead is not big enough, use a small, round jeweler's file to file open the hole and make it larger. You can also use a hand drill with a titanium bit to drill out the opening on both sides of the bead.

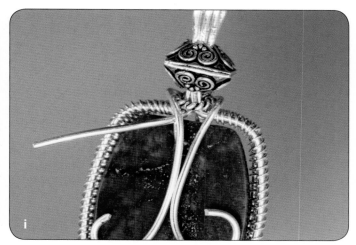

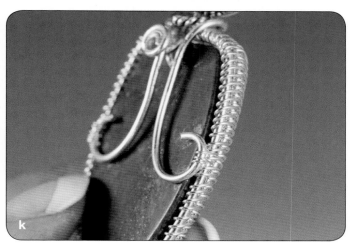

9 String the spacer bead and the bail bead over the three upright base wires. Using three-step pliers on the largest step, grasp the wires and bend them back around the tool (**h**). Keep holding them and trim all three so the ends are in the center of the bail bead. With chainnose pliers, make an upward bend in the three bail wires about ⅜ in. from the ends. This bend will help the wire catch on the inside edge of the bead to make a stronger bail.

10 Tuck all three base wires into the hole of the bail bead far enough so the bend rests on the edge of the bead. Use three-step pliers to round them out and make them uniform after they have been tucked. Swirl the two base wires that are up against the stone to touch the woven frame (**i**).

11 Make a tight Spiral (p. 22) with the last upright base wire. Place the spiral at the top of the intersection of the base wires of the weave (**j**).

12 Use the 6-in. piece of 26-gauge wire to bind the base wires to the woven frame: Poke the wire through the weave and wrap it around both the swirled base wire and the outside base wire of the weave. Trim it tightly and pinch down the ends. Do this three times to secure the base wire to the weave (**k**). Repeat on the other side to secure the stone so it will not move within the frame.

13 Create a finish with Liver of Sulfur (p. 25). Hand buff with a polishing cloth to bring out the texture in the weave.

Woven
Link
Necklace

This beautiful, adjustable necklace is accented with turquoise seed beads. The individual woven links are joined together with spiral connectors. It is based on the first half of the Flame Stitch weave so you will have lots of practice with the uphill pattern.

Materials

- 32 in. 18-gauge dead-soft copper wire
- 80 in. 20-gauge dead-soft copper wire
- 15 ft. 24-gauge dead-soft copper wire
- **11** 6° seed beads

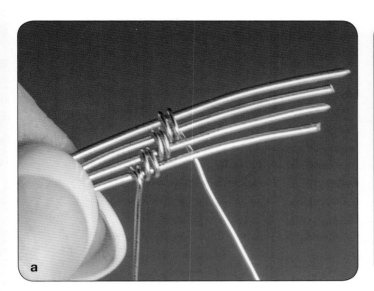

a

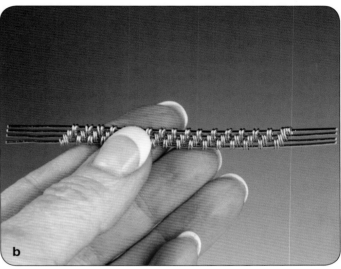

b

c

1 Cut four 4-in. pieces of 20-gauge wire for the base wires of the woven link. Cut a 3-ft. piece of 24-gauge wire for the weaving wire.

2 Complete the Uphill Wire Preparation, Double Wrap for the Flame Stitch (p. 14) with four base wires. Bring the weaving wire straight down and you are ready to begin the weave (**a**). Beginning with base wire #1, work the uphill portion of the Flame Stitch, Double Wrap (p. 17). As you reach the top of the each hill, jump down behind with the weaving wire and go directly into the uphill weave on base wire #1 again. Repeat until you have woven 2½ in. Center the weave by pulling each base wire outward with chainnose pliers. Trim the ends so you have ¼ in. of wire on each side (**b**).

3 Using three-step pliers, grasp all four wires on the end at the same time and roll them inward for medium-sized loops. Leave the loops open so you can slide the connector in place later. Do this on both ends to finish your first woven link (**c**).

d

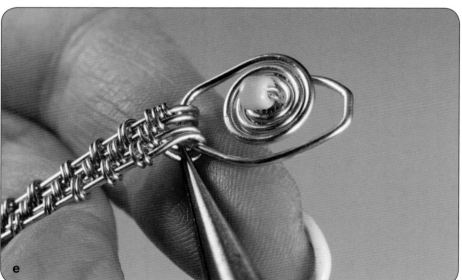

e

4 Repeat steps 2 and 3 to make a total of five woven links and set them aside. Make five Spiral Connectors (p. 23), a Gooseneck Hook (p. 20), and an extension chain (Tip) (**d**).

5 Now is the fun part: Attach all the pieces together using the connectors and the loops on the ends of the woven links (**e**). Use chainnose pliers to tighten each loop around the connector. Join all five of the woven links. You can keep the links straight or you can curve them. Customize the fit for your neck so the necklace lays smoothly down.

TIP *If you would like to add an extension chain to the necklace, link together a few more seed beads with Double-Wrapped Loops (p. 21) and add to the end of the last spiral connector.*

Intermediate Projects

Woven
Bezel
Earrings

With a simple and elegant frame, these earrings really show off a pair of beautiful stones. Here you will weave four base wires to introduce the up and downhill patterns of the Flame Stitch Weave, Single Wrap. The look is delicate and lacy, yet there is plenty of visual impact.

Materials

- 32 in. 20-gauge dead-soft sterling-silver wire
- 4 ft. 24-gauge dead-soft sterling-silver wire
- 20 in. 26-gauge dead-soft sterling-silver wire
- **2** 10x15mm amethyst cabochons
- **2** 3mm round sterling-silver beads
- pair of decorative earring posts

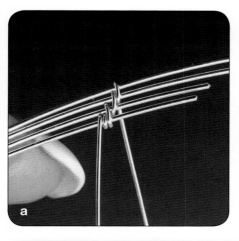

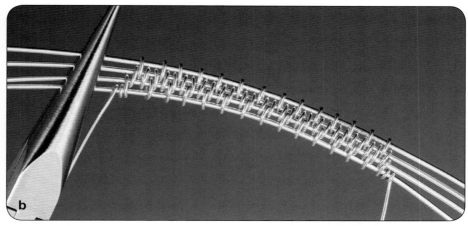

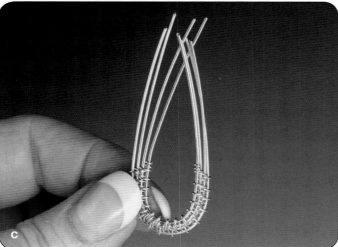

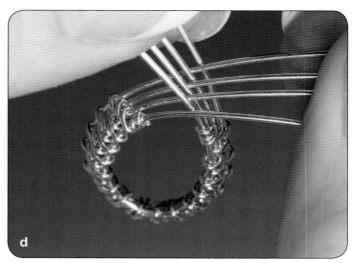

1 Cut four 4-in. pieces of 20-gauge wire for the base wires. Cut a 2-ft. piece of 24-gauge wire for the weaving wire.

2 Complete the Uphill Wire Preparation, Single Wrap (p. 13) with the four base wires (**a**).

3 Weave 1½ in. of Flame Stitch Weave (p. 16), starting with the downhill single wrap, then uphill, and then alternate between the two. One uphill and one downhill weaving pattern makes a hill. Complete 14 hills of the pattern to make a 1½-in. long weave. Center the weave on the base wires by pulling each individual base wire out with chainnose pliers. You'll have about 1½ in. on either side of the weave (**b**). Scrunch the weave tightly together.

4 Bend the weave in a U-shape that is close to the curve of one end of your stone. It doesn't have to be perfect, but try to make the curve a little smaller than the stone (**c**).

5 At the top, crisscross the base wires (p. 24), alternating left then right (**d**).

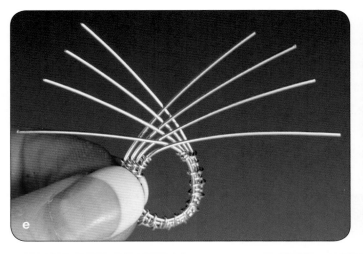

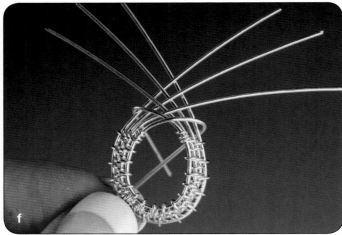

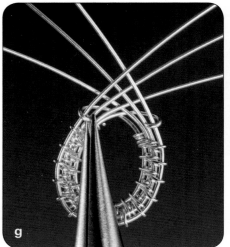

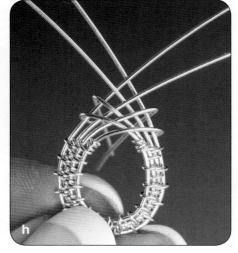

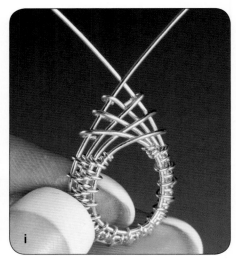

6 Starting with base wire #1 from both sides, pull each wire down to form what I call the "cathedral window." You want the wires evenly spaced and splayed out nicely (**e**).

7 Holding base wire #6 steady with your left thumb and index finger, bend base wire #1 straight back, over #6. It is important to keep the shape of the cathedral window. If you pull hard with base wire #1 as you bend it backward, it will distort the frame, making the crisscross section too small. Keep the shape of the window and hold base wire #6 steady as you bend base wire #1 around to the back. Repeat on the other side (**f**).

8 Turn the weave over and trim the ends of base wire #1 to ⅜ in. Using chainnose pliers, wrap base wire #1 around base wire #6 on each side. Make your wrap loose, to hold

the wire in place but not lock it down. It is better to start with loose wraps at first and then trim, tighten, and lock them in place later, so you get the positioning of the wire and keep the shape of the cathedral window.

Pick up the stone and place it inside the weave. You want the weave to be a little smaller around than your stone, so the stone sits inside and the weave forms a bezel to hold it in place. Adjust the loops to fit the stone. Trim the loops and tighten them to lock them in place (**g**).

9 Repeat steps 7 and 8 for base wires #2 (**h**) and #3 (**i**) on each side. Notice how the outside base wires #6 are not bending inward and that they keep the frame of the crisscross pattern at the top of the earring. It is important to do this as you make the wraps.

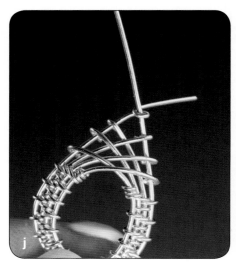

10 Make a wrap at the top of the cathedral window. Hold the two wires steady with chainnose pliers at the point where they intersect and wrap the left side base wire #6 around the right side #6 (**j**). Trim the left side #6 wire closely on the back.

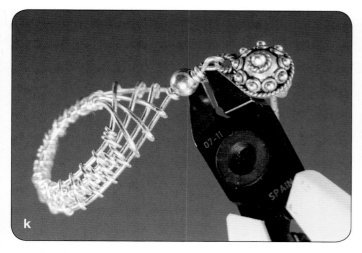

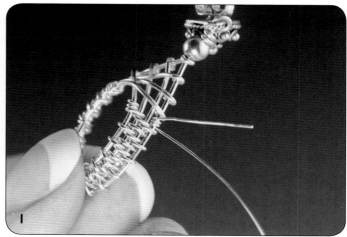

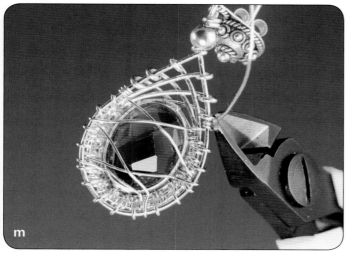

11 String a 3mm bead on the #6 base wire and make a Double-Wrapped Loop (p. 21) above the bead, connecting to the earring post before you complete the wraps. Trim the wrap closely on the back (k) and pinch it with chainnose pliers.

12 Place the stone inside the bezel and strap it in on the back: Cut a 10-in. piece of 26-gauge wire. On the left side of the weave, wrap the end of the 26-gauge wire around base wire #6 three times, right next to where the crisscross section begins (l). Trim the end close on the back.

13 Place the stone in the wire cage. Crisscross the stone with the 26-gauge wire like you are lacing up a shoe. Go back and forth five times and end on the opposite side of where you began. Wrap the 26-gauge wire three

times around the #6 base wire next to the crisscross section to mirror the wraps made in step 12. Trim the end closely (m) and pinch it down with chainnose pliers.

14 Make a second earring. Create a finish with liver of sulfur (p. 25) and buff.

For a simpler option, make the earrings through step 11. String a bead on a headpin and make a loop above the bead. Connect the loop to the bezel wire at first cross.

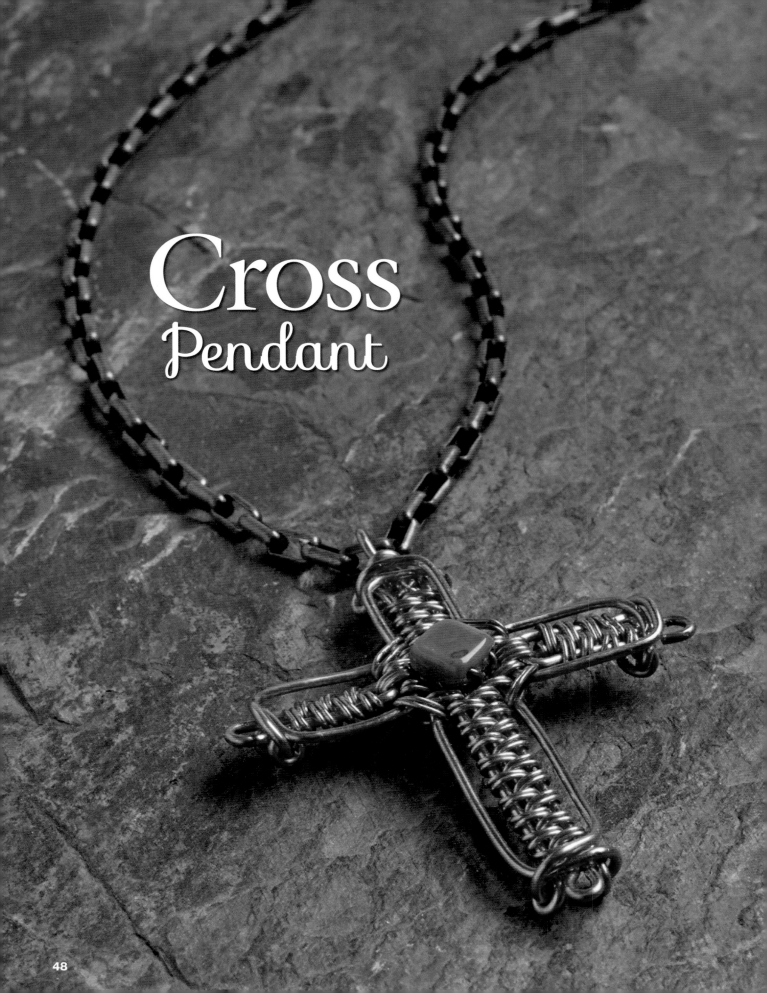

Cross
Pendant

Weave a classic cross and embellish it with a center stone or bead. The woven center is framed by 18-gauge wire, which offers a nice contrast to the texture of the weave.

Materials
- 32 in. 18-gauge dead-soft copper wire
- 66 in. 24-gauge dead-soft copper wire
- 6º seed bead and love knot spacer bead or 5mm square two-hole bead

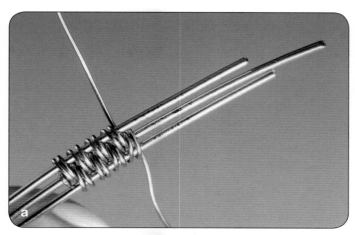

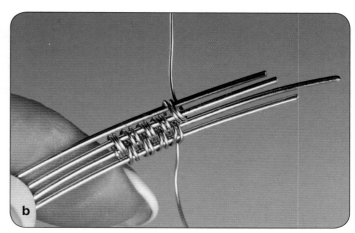

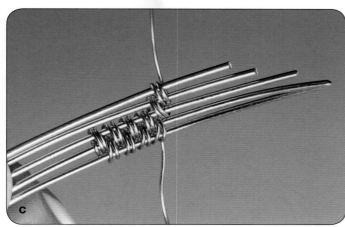

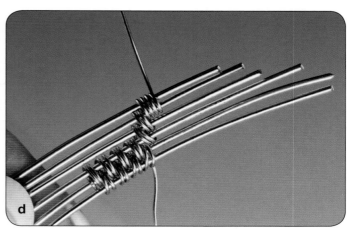

1 Cut nine 3-in. pieces of 18-gauge wire for the base wires. Cut a 3-ft. piece of 24-gauge wire for the weaving wire.

2 Begin Double Snake Weave (p. 12). Make four double wraps and stop (**a**).

3 Pick up a 3-in. piece of wire and place it on top of the weave with the weaving wire behind it. Make a double wrap around the top two wires (**b**).

4 Pick up a new 3-in. piece of wire and place it on top of the weave. Make a double wrap around the top two wires, as in step 3 (**c**).

5 Pick up a 3-in. wire and place it on top of the weave. Wrap it four times (**d**).

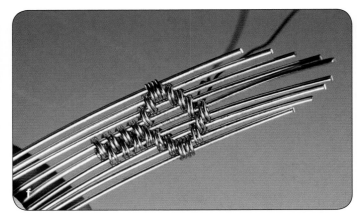

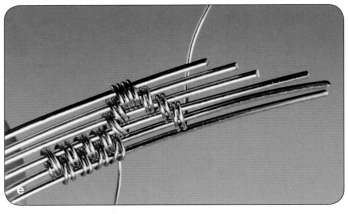

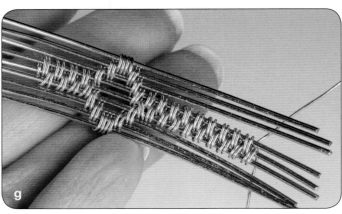

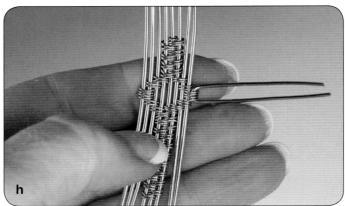

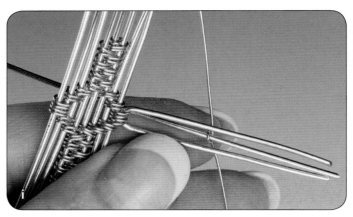

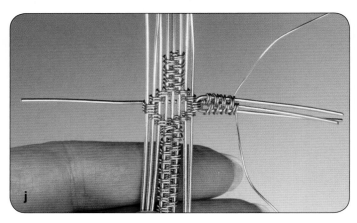

6 Weave the Downhill Flame Stitch Weave, Double Wrap (p. 18) following this pattern: Go down three wires and up two; wrap twice. Make three bundles of double wraps and stop (e).

7 Repeat steps 3–6, adding one wire and wrapping the two bottom wires twice until you have added three more wires to the weave. Wrap the bottom wire (base wire #1) four times and begin the Uphill Flame Stitch Weave, Double Wrap (p. 17). When you return to the center wire (base wire #5), wrap it twice along with base wire #4 (f).

8 Starting with the top weaving wire, weave the Double Snake Weave (p. 12) for 10 wraps (g). Center the area of the weave that has the four wraps. This is where the arms of the cross will be.

9 Take an outside base wire and bend it in a tight U-shape, like a bobby pin (h). Try to get the U in the center of the wire.

10 Cut a 10-in. piece of 24-gauge wire, fold it in half around the tip of roundnose pliers, and make a tiny loop in the center. Slide this loop on a 5-in. piece of 18-gauge wire and hold it in the center of the U-shaped base wire. Hold it so the ends are fairly even (i). This 5-in. piece will be the center base wire for the woven arm of the cross. We are sneaking in a wire that will hold both arms steady and provide the third wire necessary for the Snake Weave.

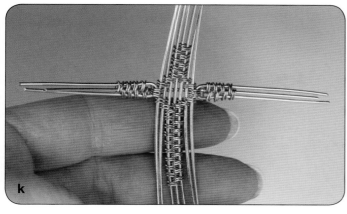

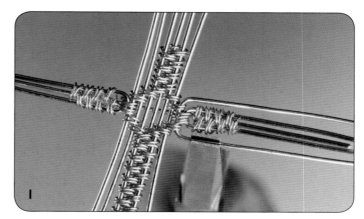

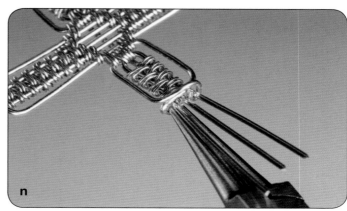

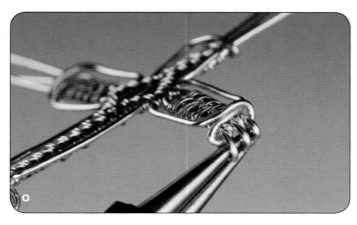

11 Begin Double Snake Weave for the first arm of the cross. Make four double wraps and stop (**j**).

12 Repeat steps 9–11 on the other side for the other woven arm of the cross (**k**).

13 Using flatnose pliers, bend the base wire next to one arm straight out at a 90-degree angle to the center section of the cross. Repeat on the other side of this arm. These wires will frame the woven section (**l**). Repeat with the other arm.

14 Make a bend right at the end of the weave on each frame wire framing the top section of the cross. Cross the wires left over right. Repeat with the bottom section of the cross and each arm (**m**).

15 Trim each of the crossed wires to ½ in. from the bend. Use roundnose pliers and make a loop around the outside wire (**n**). Trim and tighten the loops.

16 Trim all three base wires at the end of the arm to ⅜ in. Using

roundnose pliers, grasp each one and make a tight loop toward the back (**o**). Do this for both arms and the bottom section of the cross.

For the top section of the cross, cut the two outside base wires and loop them under like the others.

With the middle wire of the top arm of the cross, make a Double-Wrapped Loop for the bail (**p**) (p. 21).

51

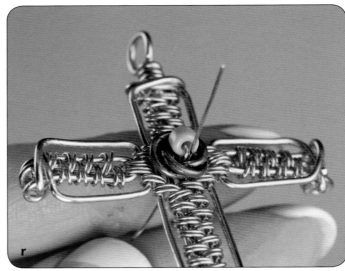

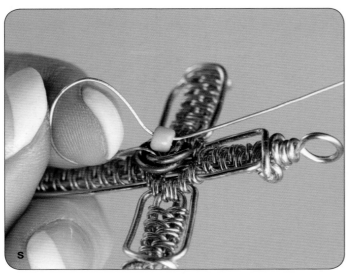

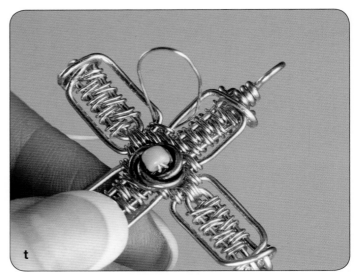

17 Cut a 10-in. piece of 24-gauge copper wire. This wire will be an add-on wire to add on the center bead embellishment. On the back, wrap the end of the add-on wire twice around the middle wire (**q**). Trim the end close and pinch it down.

18 Thread the add-on wire through the center to the front. String a two-hole bead or the love knot spacer bead and the seed bead on the wire snug to the cross. Go back through the spacer bead to the back. Come back to the front (**r**) and go back through the seed bead again and down to the back (**s**).

19 Thread the add-on wire through the space between the woven arm and the wire that frames

The silver cross has an extra bead at each end secured by a loop; the copper cross features a seed bead in the center.

v

it (**t**). Pull the wire tight and go back through the next arm's space between the woven section and the framing wire. Pull the wire tight to make two wraps on the back, and pull the wire across to the next arm. Wrap each framing wire twice to the one next to it on all sides (**u**). This will stabilize the arms of the cross and they will not move.

20 Tie off the add-on wire by making two wraps around the center wire, right next to where you started. Trim this wire tightly (**v**) and pinch down the end.

21 To create a finish and bring out the texture of the weave, apply liver of sulfur (p. 25) and buff.

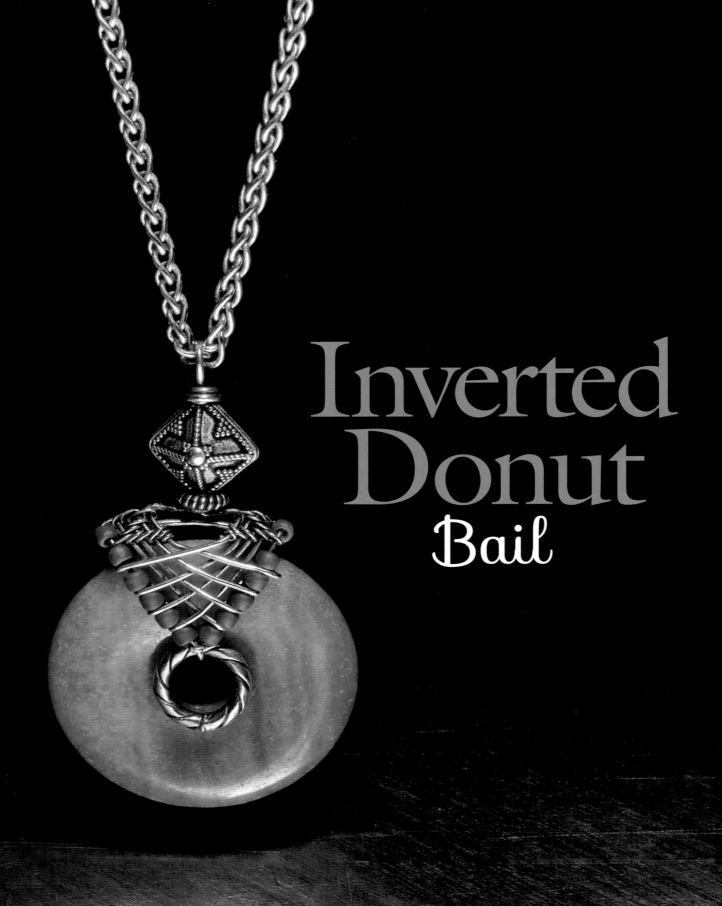

Inverted Donut Bail

This exotic and unusual bail for a donut-shaped stone is derived from many of the same techniques we have been working with. Weave with five base wires and one weaving wire. Add seed beads for some color. This project makes a very pretty shape that complements the circular lines of the stone.

Materials

- 5 in. 18-gauge dead-soft sterling-silver wire
- 25 in. 20-gauge dead-soft sterling-silver wire
- 24 in. 24-gauge dead-soft sterling-silver wire
- 40mm donut-shaped focal stone
- **21 8º seed beads**
- 10mm bead (for the bail)
- spacer bead with large hole
- circle half of a toggle clasp with loop removed

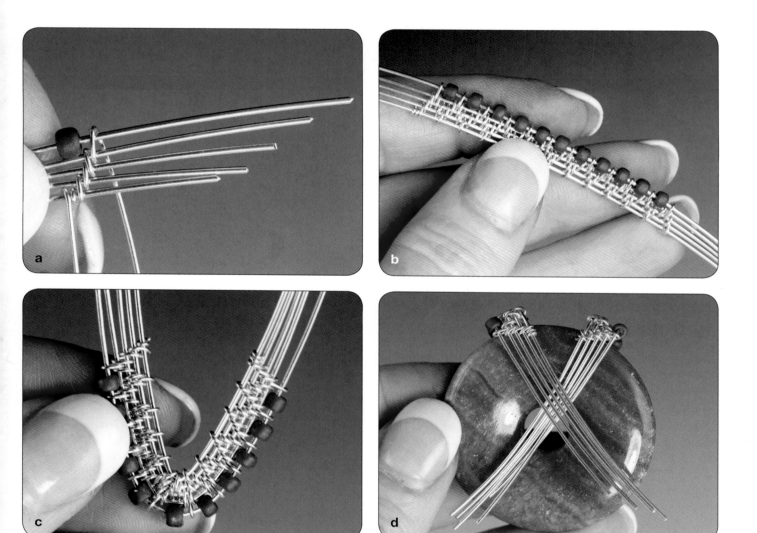

1 Cut five 5-in. pieces of 20-gauge wire for the base wires. Use the 24-gauge wire for the weaving wire.

2 Complete the Uphill Wire Preparation, Single Wrap (p. 13). As you come to base wire #5, string an 8º seed bead on the wire (**a**).

3 Weave 2 in. of Uphill and Downhill Flame Stitch Weave, Single Wrap (p. 16), adding one seed bead on base wire #5 every time you go over the top of a hill (**b**). Wrap the weaving wire around base wire #1 three times and trim to finish the end. Remove the seed bead from step 2 and center the weave on the base wires.

4 Make a flat V in the weave with the centered weave and the beads on the outside edge (**c**).

5 Using the stone as a guide, place the weave on the back and hold it while you bend each end of the wires over the edge and onto the front. The open ends will cross (**d**).

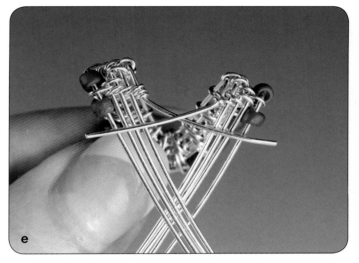

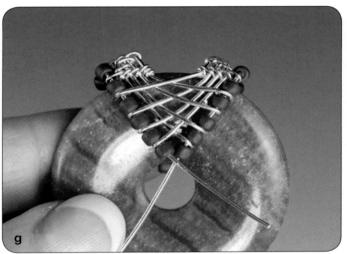

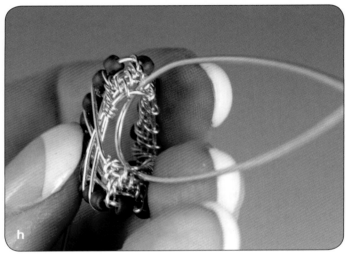

6 Set the stone aside. String one seed bead on each side of base wire #5. Pull out base wire #1 on the left and place it on top of all the base wires on the right. Pick up base wire #1 on the right and place it on top of all the base wires on the left. Trim these wires so that they extend ⅜ in. longer than the outside base wire edge (e).

7 Using chainnose pliers, turn the end of the trimmed crossed wires around base wire #5, making a small loop around the base wire right next to the seed bead (f). Repeat on the other side.

8 Repeat steps 6 and 7, adding beads, crossing the wires, trimming, and tucking until you come to the last two wires—base wires #5 (g).

9 Bend a 5-in. piece of 18-gauge wire in a big U shape. Coming from inside the weave, thread the ends of this U-shaped wire through the top of the weave and pull it until it is centered (h). You may need to open up space for this wire with a T-pin. Leave the 18-gauge wire there for now.

10 Wrap one of the #5 base wires around the other #5. Make a single wrap and trim it close on the back (**i**). Pinch the cut end with chainnose pliers.

11 Place the toggle circle on the remaining base wire #5. Bend the base wire #5 so that it goes through the hole from front to back (**j**).

12 Cut the base wire #5 about ⅜ in. longer than where it intersects with the back portion of the weave. Make a small bend in this wire around the weave in the back. Pinch down the bend so it makes a hook that holds the two sections together (**k**).

13 Bend the 18-gauge wires extending from the top inward toward each other. Bend one straight up, in the middle. Center this wire (it will hold the bail bead). I never get things in the middle the first time. It may take a few tries, but don't give up. Wrap the other 18-gauge wire around the one that is straight up once. Trim this wire on the back and pinch it down tight (**l**).

14 String the spacer bead and the 10mm bead on the upright 18-gauge wire and make a large Double-Wrapped Loop (p. 21) above the beads (**m**). Remember to orient the loop perpendicular to the weaving so that the chain will slide through in the right direction.

Scalloped Edge
Woven Bracelet

The main weave for this elegant bracelet is the Double Snake Weave, which requires three main base wires with one shared in the middle. Designs with this weave as the main pattern must use a number of base wires that is divisible by three for a balanced look. Here there are nine base wires: three on top, three in the middle that share the center wire, and three on the bottom. The scalloped edges are hammered for strength and for looks, and the diamond shapes formed in the weaving pattern are highlighted by the embellishment. You'll learn a lot by making this bracelet.

Materials
- 3 in. 18-gauge dead-soft copper wire
- 6 ft. 20-gauge dead-soft copper wire
- 8½ ft. 24-gauge dead-soft copper wire
- **16** 8º seed beads

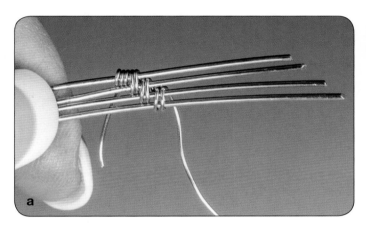

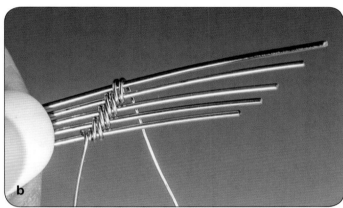

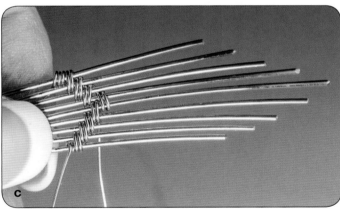

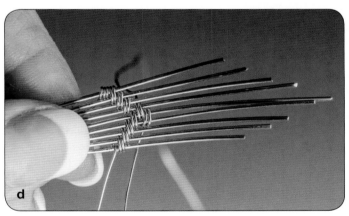

1 Cut seven 7½-in. and two 9½-in. pieces of 20-gauge wire for the base wires. Cut two 3½-ft. pieces of 24-gauge wire for the top and bottom weaving wires.

2 Using one of the 9½-in. base wires for the top base wire (base wire #9) and three of the 7½-in. base wires, prepare the top section for wire weaving by completing the Downhill Wire Preparation, Double Wrap (p. 15) **(a)**. Set this bundle down.

3 Pick up the four remaining 7½-in. and a 9½-in. base wires. Place the longest wire on the bottom (base wire #1) and the other four lined up above this one. Complete the Uphill Wire Preparation, Double Wrap (p. 14) for these five base wires **(b)**.

4 Pick up the bundle from step 2 and place it on top of the bundle from step 3. Base wire #5 is the shared wire for this pattern. I like to pull it out a little farther than the others so I can

identify it easily. Use the weaving wire from the top and wrap twice around base wires #5 and #6 **(c)**.

5 Wrap the bottom weaving wire twice around base wires #4 and #5 **(d)**. Begin the Double Snake Weave (p. 12) wrapping twice from both sides, alternating as you go.

TIP Position the base wires in steps like a ladder so you can easily see which wire is which.

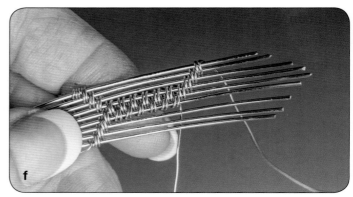

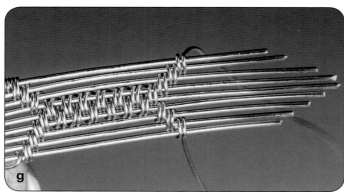

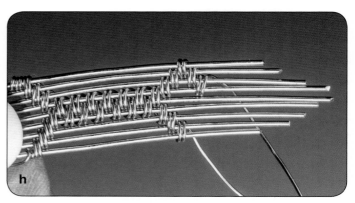

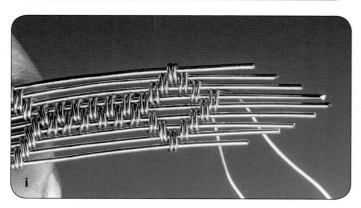

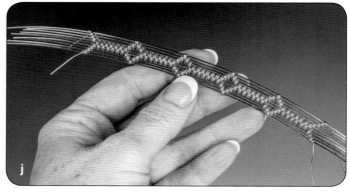

6 Weave the Double Snake Weave seven times on the three middle wires, base wires #4, #5, and #6, alternating the weaving wires for each double wrap (**e**). As you need more weaving space on the base wires, slide each one out about 1 in. by grasping with chainnose pliers and pulling.

7 The weave will now separate and create the diamond shape. For the top section, use the top weaving wire: Wrap twice around base wires #6 and #7 and come up between them. Wrap twice around base wires #7 and #8 and come up between them. Wrap twice around base wires #8 and #9 and stop there (**f**). For the bottom section,

come through from behind and direct the weaving wire between base wires #2 and #3. Wrap base wires #3 and #4 twice. Jump down from behind and come up between base wires #1 and #2, and wrap #2 and #3 twice. Jump down, come from behind, and wrap base wires #1 and #2 twice (**g**).

8 Bring the two sections of the weave back together. Start with the top weaving wire, jump down from behind, come up between base wires #6 and #7, and wrap twice around base wires #7 and #8. Jump down from behind again, come between base wires #5 and #6, and wrap twice around base wires #6 and #7 (**h**).

9 To complete the diamond shape, bring the lower section to meet the top. Start by bringing the weaving wire between base wires #1 and #2, and then wrap twice around base wires #2 and #3. Come between base wires #2 and #3 and wrap twice around base wires #3 and #4. Come between base wires #3 and #4 and wrap twice around base wires #4 and #5 (**i**). Start the Double Snake Weave again, starting with the top weaving wire and wrapping twice around #5 and #6.

10 Repeat steps 5–9 to weave a total of four complete diamond shapes. At the fifth diamond, stop at the top and wrap twice around the

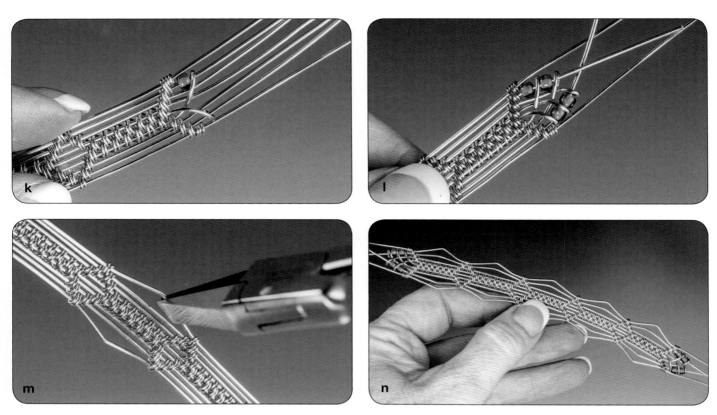

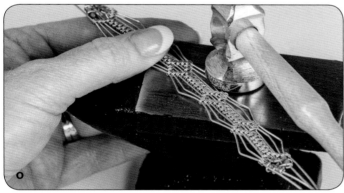

outside base wire. Trim the weaving wires closely on the back and pinch tight with chainnose pliers. Repeat with the lower section. Center the weave by pulling out each wire with chainnose pliers until they are even (**j**).

11 Since this weave has an odd number of base wires, the crisscross end will not be quite symmetrical. To compensate, start the Crisscross Finished End (p. 24) by stringing a seed bead on base wire #8 (**k**). Do not string one on base wire #2. Complete the end as in crisscross finished end.

12 Crisscross left over right, wrapping the crossed wires around base wires #2 and #8. Wrap each end, trim, and tighten the crossed wire. String a seed bead between the crossed wires. Repeat on the other side (**l**).

13 Using flatnose pliers, pull out the center of the outside base wires (#1 and #9) in between the diamond shapes to make an angled bend (**m**). Start in the middle and work your way to the outside on each end.

14 Go back to each section and use your thumb and index finger to pull out the next base wires (#8 and #2). Make a slight arch in them, a softer version of what you just did (**n**).

15 Hammer the two outside wires with a chasing hammer against a bench block or hard surface (**o**). This strengthens them and adds a beautiful shine and texture.

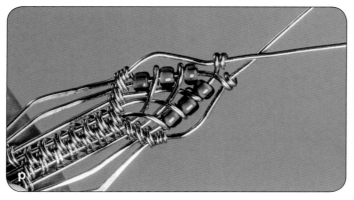

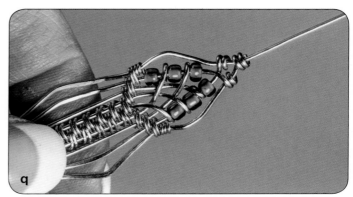

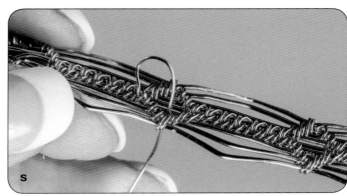

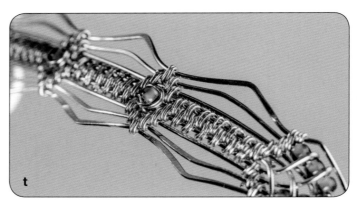

16 Wrap base wire #2 around base wire #9 twice, trim, and pinch it down (**p**). Wrap base wire #8 around base wire #1 twice and pinch it down. Wrap base wire #1 around base wire #9 twice, trim, and pinch down (**q**).

17 Make a Double-Wrapped Loop (p. 21) on the end of the remaining base wire. Wrap it around itself twice and trim it tightly on the back (**r**). Pinch the end down.

18 Add seed beads to the center of each diamond shape (**s, t**) and give each seed bead a Turtleneck (p. 19).

19 Make a Gooseneck Hook (p. 20) and attach it to one of the loops on the end (**u**). Mold the bracelet to fit your wrist.

TIP This pattern makes a 6½-in. woven section. The Gooseneck Hook (p. 20) (u) adds another ½ in. to the length so the bracelet ends up to be about 7¼-in. long. You can always make a bigger hook and add length to your finished piece.

Advanced
Projects

Woven Bezel
Pendant

Weaving a bezel around a focal stone is a classic and adaptable design. The stone can be a cabochon or a large, flat vertically drilled bead. Choose a smooth stone without much texture. The bezel adds a lot of visual interest; it should enhance the stone, not compete with it.

This design can be adapted to any size stone, but it is best to start out learning with a medium-sized stone (around 25mm) that is oval or pear shaped. Other sizes and shapes are good for challenging you when you have had some practice.

Materials

- 32 in. 20-gauge dead-soft copper wire
- 4½ ft. 24-gauge dead-soft copper wire
- 25mm stone cabochon or bead, oval or pear shape
- 8mm round copper bead with 3mm hole
- large-hole spacer bead
- **25** 8º seed beads

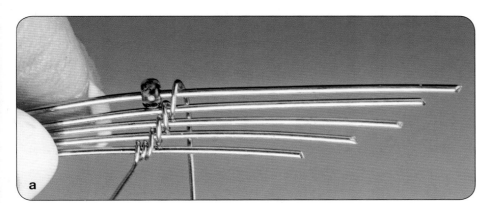

a

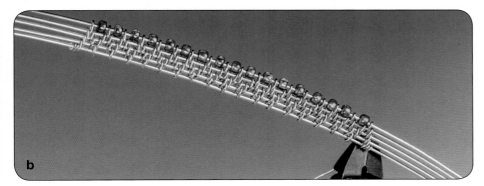

b

c

TIP To determine how long to cut your base wires if your stone differs from mine, measure the circumference of your stone with a piece of string. Add 3 in. for the length needed for each base wire.

1 Cut five 6¼-in. pieces of 20-gauge wire for the base wires. Cut a 3-ft. piece of 24-gauge wire for the weaving wire.

2 Complete the Uphill Wire Preparation, Single Wrap (p. 13) on five base wires. When you are adding base wire #5, string an 8º seed bead to the left of the weaving wire as you go over the first hill (a).

3 Weave 18 hills of Flame Stitch Weave, alternating Downhill and Uphill Single Wrap (p. 16), for about 2¾ in. of weave, depending on how tightly you scrunch. This stone measures 3¼ in. around, so I wove a section that is 2¾ in. long—½-in. shorter than the circumference of the stone—to allow room at the top for the crisscross finishing.
 Center the weave on the base wires by pulling each one individually with chainnose pliers. Wrap the weaving wire three times around base wire #1 and trim it tightly on the back (b).

4 Bend the centered weave in a U-shape to resemble the bottom of your stone. It doesn't have to be perfect, just similar (c). You will be fitting the stone later.

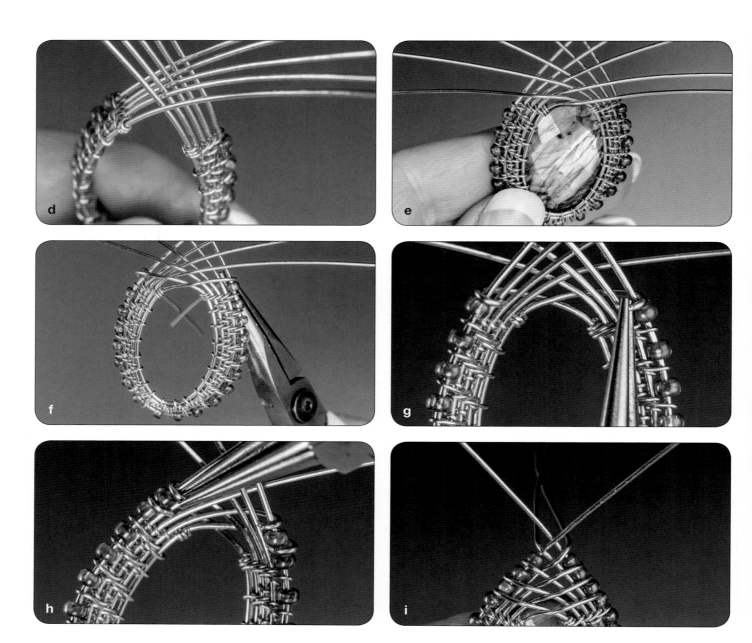

5 Crisscross the base wires, starting with the left and alternating (**d**).

6 To fit the stone, begin by pulling base wires #1 down so that they almost touch the woven area. Bring base wires #2 down and then base wires #3 and base wires #4 so that they splay outward and form what I call the "cathedral window." Fitting is important, so you want to mold the weave to hug the outside edge of the stone (**e**).

7 String a seed bead on each base wire #5. Carefully bend both base wires #1 around base wires #5. Try not to pull too hard. You don't want to distort the shape of the cathedral window (**f**). This is the hardest part of the whole piece. Try to keep the shape as you bend the base wires over and to the back.

8 Turn the piece over and trim both the base wires #1 to ⅜ in. Using chainnose pliers, bend the ends around the base wires #5 loosely (**g**). Don't tighten them yet; you have to do a final fitting. Just make an approximate loop and leave it at that.

9 Repeat steps 7 and 8 on base wires #2 and #3 (**h**). Work in pairs: It is easier to keep the symmetry if the wires are bent in pairs instead of alternating sides.

10 When you get to base wires #4, bend them straight back but do not cut them (**i**). They will be used for the bail so you need the length of the full wire on both sides.

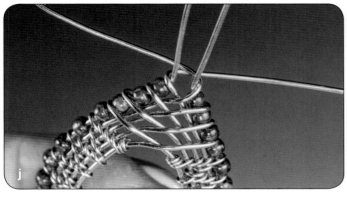

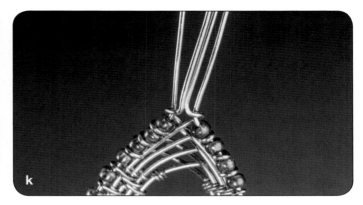

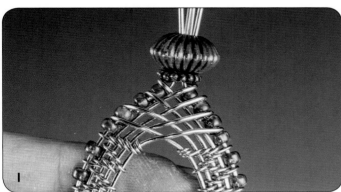

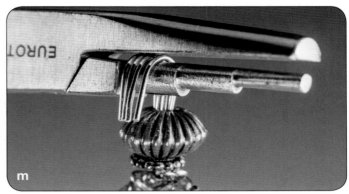

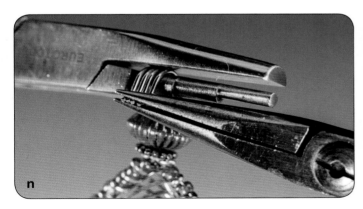

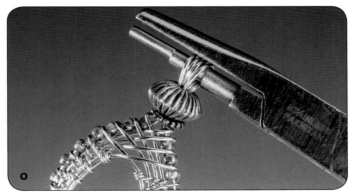

11 Cross both base wires #4 in the back. Bend the base wires #5 straight up so they do not cross (**j**).

12 On the back, using chainnose pliers, grasp each of the base wires #4 at the intersection and bend them straight up (**k**).

13 String the spacer bead and the 8mm round bead over all four base wires (**l**). (These wires will become the bail.)

NOTE If your bead is not sitting straight, check the angle of the base wires #4 where they were bent backwards. Often these are the culprits if your bail bead is crooked. If so, remove the beads and tweak the wires until they bend equally and make a flat foundation for the bail beads.

14 Using three-step pliers, grasp all four bail wires and bend them back over the largest step of the pliers. Trim all four wires with wire cutters at the same time, so that the ends are about halfway down the side of the bead (**m**). This ensures enough wire to tuck inside the bail bead to form the bail.

15 Hold the four bail wires with three-step pliers in your left hand and use chainnose pliers to make a ⅜ in. bend in all four bail wires (**n**). Grasp the ends and pull up on all four at the same time to ensure a uniform size.

16 Using chainnose pliers, grasp each wire separately at the bend you just made, lift it up, and tuck it into the hole of the 8mm bail bead. Repeat with the remaining bail wires. Don't worry if they are crooked—that's normal. Once you have them all tucked in, use the second step of the three-step pliers to pinch them down in a smooth circle for the bail (**o**).

17 Make a coiled wire back (see p. 69 for a beaded back option) to hold the stone inside the back of the piece: Start by cutting a 4- and a 3-in. piece of 20-gauge wire. Bend the 4-in. piece in a large swirl on one side and a small swirl on the other. With the 3-in. piece, make two small swirls. Bind the two together with a 6-in. piece of 24-gauge wire in the middle, making five wraps. Place this on the back of the piece and tighten the swirls to fit more closely to the stone. It is good if they are a little big, as pictured (**p**).

18 Using the rest of the 24-gauge wire, bind the swirls to the woven bezel by threading the end between base wires #4 and #5 at the beginning of the weave. Make two wraps and trim both ends tightly. Pinch down the ends (**q**).

19 Repeat step 18 at all the places the swirls touch the outside of the woven bezel. You can also bind the swirls to each other if they touch (**r**). This will strengthen the design.

20 Create a finish with liver of sulfur (p. 25) and buff with a polishing cloth.

Beaded Back Option for the Woven Bezel Pendant

Who doesn't love variety? Here's an option for finishing the back of a Woven Bezel Pendant. Bead the back for an unexpected look that makes the pendant completely reversible. The pattern of the beadwork resembles the pattern of the Flame Stitch Weave and is adaptable to any size stone.

Materials
- Woven Bezel Pendant with stone through step 16
- 2 yd. Fireline 4 lb. test
- **77** 11º Color A seed beads
- **75** 11º Color B seed beads
- **50** 15º Color C seed beads

Tools
- #12 embroidery needle
- wire cutters

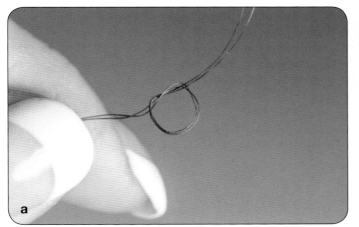

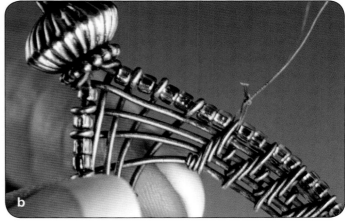

1 Cut 2 yd. of Fireline. Center the needle on the thread.

2 Make a small knot on the end of the Fireline (**a**). Trim the end next to the knot with wire cutters.

3 Secure the Fireline to the bezel by stitching through the top loop of the first hill of the Flame Stitch. Bring the needle between the threads and pull it tight (**b**).

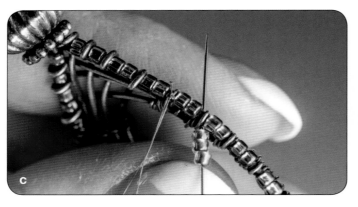

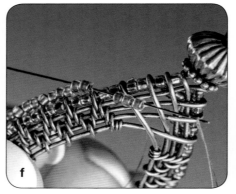

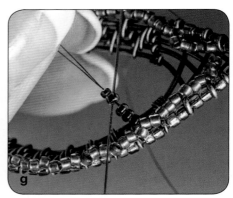

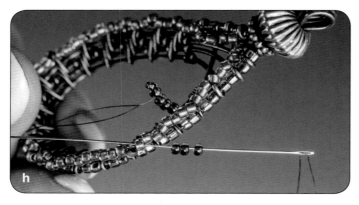

4 Pick up three color B 11º seed beads. Stitch through the next top loop in the woven bezel (c).

5 Bring the needle under the double thread, right next to the beads just strung (d). This will keep the beads from twisting.

6 Continue around the edge of the bezel, repeating steps 4 and 5 of adding three Bs, going through the wire weave, and going back under the thread. When you come to the top, make the jump across the bail in the same manner: Pick up three Bs and stitch through the center section of the crisscross (e). Continue until you reach the starting place (figure 1). This makes the foundation of the woven back.

7 When you return to the starting point, sew through the first two beads of the group of three to position the thread for the next section (photo f and figure 1, point c).

8 Pick up three color A 11º seed beads and one 15º seed bead. Push them up to the frame. Skip the 15º and sew back through the closest 11º. Hold the beads in place with your left thumb and index finger as you pull the thread taut (g).

9 Pick up three As and sew through the sixth bead in line (h). (This is the center bead of the second group of beads that you sewed in the foundation.)

10 Pull the thread tight. See the pattern emerging in the beads with the 15º bead on top (photo i and figure 2).

11 Continue all the way around the line of foundation beads. When you return to the starting point, sew up through the first side of the beads and through the 15º (j). Pull the thread tight.

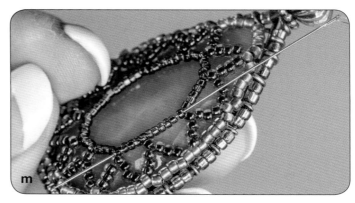

Figure 1

Figure 2

Figure 3

12 Pick up five 15ºs and sew through the next 15º (**k**). You will be jumping across, placing beads between to connect each point at the 15ºs.

13 Continue adding the 15ºs to jump across. As you go around the curve, you do not need as many 15ºs to make the jump; add only the number that is needed (**l**). Here I started by adding five, then four, then three as I went around the curve. As

the shape of the stone straightened, I needed to add a few more to make the jump. Every stone can be different, so you can decide how many beads are needed to make up for the curves of your stone.

14 Sew all the way around, adding 15ºs to jump from 15º to 15º. When you return to the starting place, sew through the beads again (**m**). Make a full circle. This strengthens the design (**figure 3**).

TIP I sew through the entire design to add more strength and to tighten it up. This is optional, but I highly recommend you do it. The beads will line up with each other better and the whole thing will look more professional.

Double Diamond
Woven Bracelet

This design is the most versatile in this collection. There are 16 base wires, including two heavy framing wires that add strength and beauty. Two independent weaving wires interconnect in the center, forming diamond shapes in the pattern. As they interconnect, they share the two central base wires. Because this weave makes its pattern in bundles of two wires, an even number of base wires is required. Mix up the design for your own pattern by adding or subtracting base wires (keeping an even number). The wire accent on top of the turquoise beads adds attractive detail.

Materials
- 28 in. 14-gauge dead-soft copper wire
- 9 ft. 20-gauge dead-soft copper wire
- 10 ft. 24-gauge dead-soft copper wire
- **3** 12mm square beads, diagonally drilled
- **24** 8º seed beads

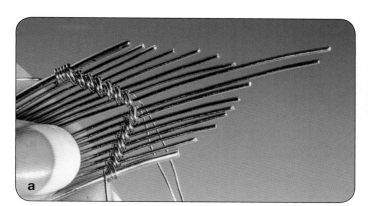

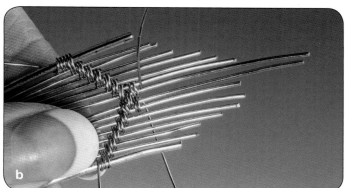

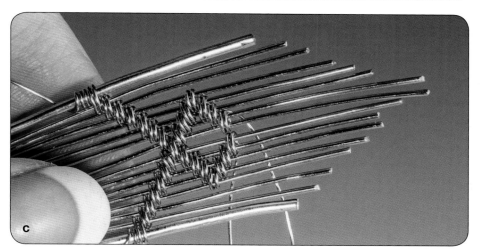

1 Cut two 9-in. pieces of 14-gauge wire for the outside edges or framing wire. Cut 14 7½ in. pieces of 20-gauge wire for the base wires. Cut two 3½ ft. pieces of 24-gauge wire for the weaving wires.

2 With seven 20-gauge base wires and the framing wire on the outside edge (top), prepare for weaving with the Downhill Wire Preparation, Double Wrap (p. 15). This is the top portion of the weave. With the remaining seven base wires and the framing wire on the outside edge (bottom), begin the Uphill Wire Preparation, Double Wrap (p. 14). This is the bottom portion of the weave. Pick both sections up and hold them as pictured (**a**).

NOTE Notice how I have pulled the two middle (shared) wires out a little farther than the others. This makes them easy to see so you know where to place the weaving wire.

3 Interconnect the Top and Bottom Weaves (p. 18). Remember to leave a bit more space in the middle, between the two center wires, for the weaving wires to double up on each other (**b**).

4 On the top section, weave the Uphill Flame Stitch, Double Wrap (p. 17) for four stitches with the top weaving wire. Weave Downhill Flame Stitch, Double Wrap (p. 18) for four stitches. On the bottom section, using the bottom weaving wire, weave Downhill Flame Stitch, Double Wrap for four stitches. Weave Uphill Flame Stitch, Double Wrap for four stitches. The two portions should meet in the middle, at the two shared central base wires with both weaving wires behind (**c**).

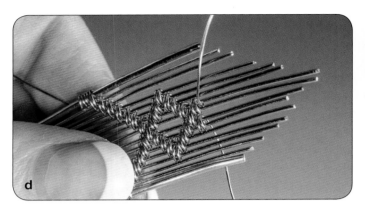

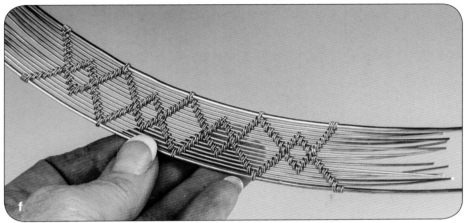

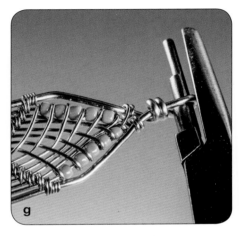

5 Interconnect the top and bottom weave as you did in step 3 (d).

NOTE As you are weaving, you'll reach the edge of the base wires and you'll want more room. Slide the weave to the left by pulling on each individual base wire with chainnose pliers until you have about 1 in. on the right side of your weave (e). Continue weaving.

6 Continue the pattern of weaving Uphill Flame Stitch on the top portion to the top framing wire and then immediately downhill to the center. Weave the mirror image on the bottom portion with Downhill Flame Stitch to the framing wire and back uphill to meet the top weave in the center.

7 The full woven pattern for the design is pictured (f). When your weave is completed, wrap the weaving wires three times around the outside framing wire. Trim on the back tightly and pinch the ends down with chainnose pliers.

Center the weave by pulling out each individual base wire with chainnose pliers. This weave is 4¼-in.

long, so there should be about 1½ in. of base wire on each side and about 2¾ in. of framing wires on each side. If your weave is a little longer than this, it's fine. There is still plenty of wire to complete the crisscross finishing. Better to have too much wire than not enough. You can always scrunch your weave to condense it for a smaller bracelet.

8 Finish each end with the Crisscross Finishing Technique (p. 24). Make a Double-Wrapped Loop at each end (p. 21)(g).

TIP If you find that your stitches are not always in a nice, diagonal line, use chainnose pliers and pinch them into alignment. Pinch the whole row at once and they will line up properly.

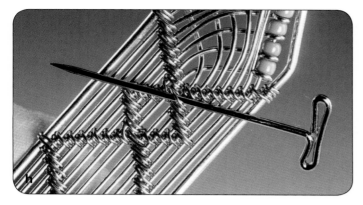

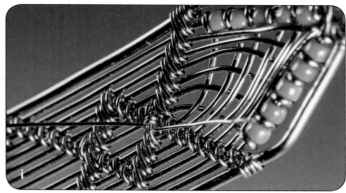

9 The weaving is completed, so now we move to the fun part: adding embellishments. On the back of your bracelet, in the intersection of the two weaving wires, there will be a longer wire in the weaving pattern. Poke a T-pin behind that wire, and wriggle it around, opening up a space for other wires to pass through (**h**). Do this to all the intersections on the back of the bracelet.

10 Cut a 3-ft. piece of 24-gauge add-on wire. On the back of the bracelet, wrap the end of the add-on wire around the loop you opened up at the base of the right crisscross section twice (**i**). Trim the end tightly and pinch it down with chainnose pliers.

11 Thread the add-on wire through the center of the first small diamond shape from the back to the front. String an 8° seed bead on the wire and give it a Turtleneck (p. 19) in the center of the diamond. Push the add-on wire to the back through the center and make sure the wire is tight. On the back, thread the add-on wire through the next loop that you opened with the T-pin and back through the middle of the next diamond shape to the front. String one of the turquoise beads on the add-on wire and push it to the front of the bracelet. Thread the wire back through the center and through the next opened loop in the weave (**j**).

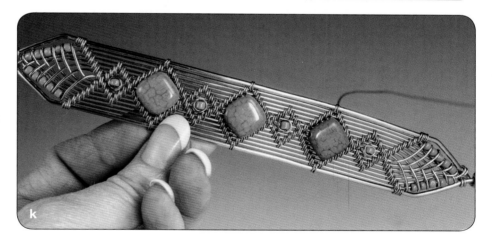

12 Repeat twice for a total of four turtlenecked beads and three 12mm beads (**k**).

> NOTE The bracelet could be finished right now if you want, but we won't stop. Let's add more embellishment.

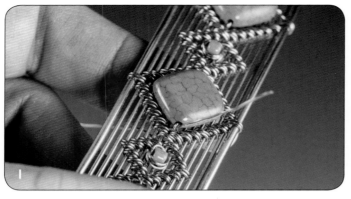

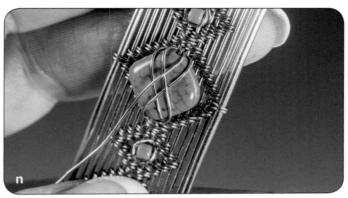

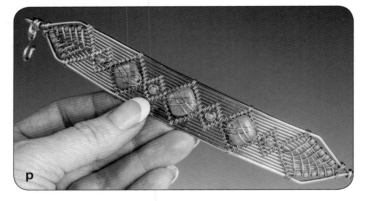

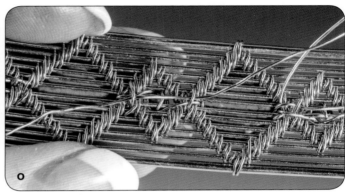

13 Pass the add-on wire through the center, right next to the 12mm bead from back to front. Pull the wire tight (**l**).

14 Make a figure-8 shape with the add-on wire by going across the stone, tucking the wire under the wire that is holding the 12mm bead in place, and pulling the wire tight. Go across the stone again, crisscrossing the wires on top of the stone. Thread the add-on wire under the wire that holds the stone and pull the wire tight (**m**). Push the area in the figure 8 wider on the right side with your fingers. The next figure 8 will loop inside the larger end of the figure 8.

15 Bring the add-on wire across the stone again so that the wire lays inside the larger side of the figure eight. Push the add-on wire under the wire that holds the stone again and come across the bead, making a small loop that sits inside the first loop (**n**).

16 Pass the add-on wire through the center to the back, next to the 12mm bead, and pull the wire tight. Jump to the next intersection where you opened a loop with the T-pin. Pass the add-on wire through that loop and the next one, jumping over the small diamond shape (**o**). This takes the add-on wire right to the next 12mm bead.

17 Direct the wire through the center to the front, on the right side of the next 12mm bead, and repeat steps 13–16 until all three 12mm beads have wire accents.

18 Make a Gooseneck Hook (p. 20) and slide it on one of the loops at the crisscross ends (**p**).

19 Mold the bracelet in a curve to fit your wrist.

Mirror Image
Bracelet

This bracelet is the largest, with 16 base wires and four independent weaving wires. Although it has four weaving wires, we will only weave two at a time, creating two separate sections which make the design more manageable. We'll "stitch" the two halves together with the seed beads as embellishment.

Materials
- 19 in. 14-gauge dead-soft copper wire
- 9½ ft. 20-gauge dead-soft copper wire
- 18 ft. 24-gauge dead-soft copper wire
- **8** large-hole spacers
- **8** 6º seed beads
- **20** 8º seed beads

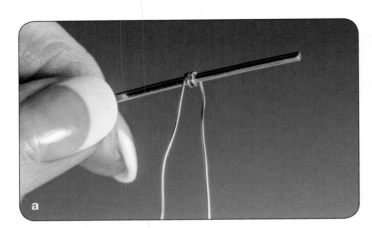

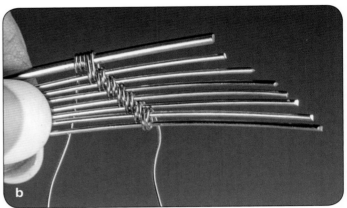

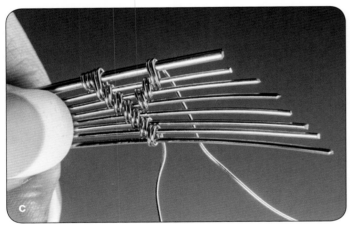

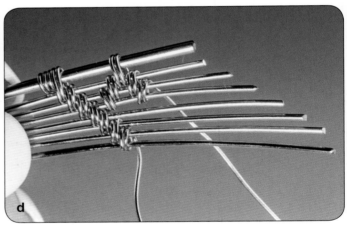

1 Cut two 9½-in. pieces of 14-gauge wire for the outside frame. Cut 14 8-in. pieces of 20-gauge wire for the base wires. Cut two 9-ft. pieces of 24-gauge wire for the weaving wires.

2 Measure 6 ft. on a 9-ft. weaving wire and make a bend at that spot. Pick up a 14-gauge wire (the top wire of this portion of the bracelet: base wire #8). Place the base wire inside the bend of the weaving wire, with the shorter part in front and longer part in back, and wrap the longer end of the weaving wire around the base wire three times (**a**).

3 Complete the Downhill Wire Preparation, Double Wrap (p. 15) for a total of eight wires. Both weaving wires are on the back side of the piece when this is done (**b**).

4 Start weaving again with the shorter weaving wire. Pull it between base wires #4 and #5. Wrap base wire #4 and base wire #5 twice and come up between them. Continue with the uphill Flame Stitch Weave, Double Wrap (**p. 17**) until you are at the top, on base wire #8 (**c**).

5 Continue weaving and go right into the Downhill Flame Stitch Weave, Double Wrap (p. 18) for three stitches. Notice how you have made a small, upside down V with the shorter weaving wire. This is the only pattern you will weave with this wire. Stop there for now (**d**).

As you need space for weaving, pull each base wire out with chainnose pliers so that there is about 1 in. of wire showing.

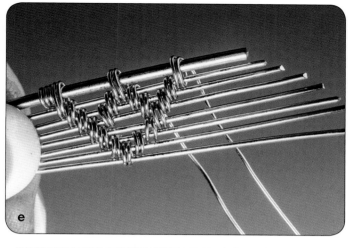

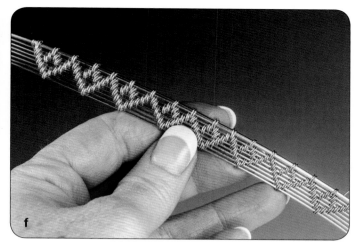

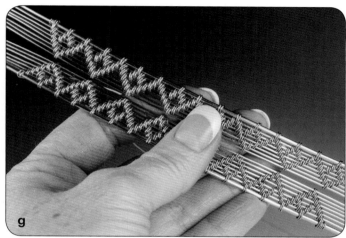

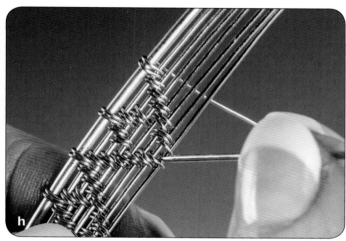

6 Return to the longer weaving wire and begin the Uphill Flame Stitch Weave right next to the last stitch you made with it. Bring the weaving wire between base wires #1 and #2 and begin weaving. Go all the way up to the top of the hill on base wire #8 (e). Notice how you have made a large V that goes to the outside of the small upside down V within it. This large V is the only pattern you will weave with the longer weaving wire.

7 Repeat the pattern seven more times: Weave Downhill Flame Stitch with the longer weaving wire from #8 to the bottom of the hill. Go to the shorter weaving wire, start between base wires #4 and #5, and weave three stitches in the uphill pattern to the top. Go directly into the downhill weave for two stitches.

Go back to the longer weaving wire to complete the large V by weaving the uphill pattern, starting between base wires #1 and #2 and going all the way up to the top of the hill, finishing at base wire #8 (f).

8 Repeat steps 2–7 to make the second half of the bracelet. You'll have two identical pieces. Turn one of the pieces 180 degrees for a mirror image. The 14-gauge wires will both be on the outside edges. Match up the weave point to point (g). Scrunch the weave to move it to fit the best you can. It does not have to be perfect; close will do. You can see mine does not fit perfectly but it works out fine in the end. Trim both ends of the shorter weaving wire on the backside closely, but leave the longer weaving wires attached. Use these wires to add the embellishments.

9 Using a T-pin, open up a space between the two stitches on each point on base wire #1 (h). Do this to all of the points on the second section.

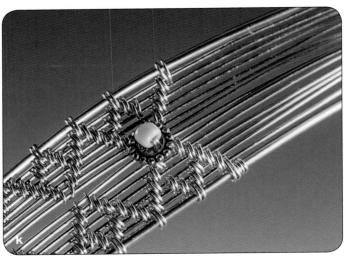

TIP Remember to loop the wire around your finger every time you pull the wire to make a stitch. Wire will want to kink so keep the lines of the wire in smooth curves so it will slide through the beads.

10 Using the long weaving wire, connect the two sections by pushing the weaving wire from behind at the spot you just opened with the T-pin on the left, come over in front, and go down through the other opened spot on the second section (**i**). Pull the wire tight, and the two sections will join to form one piece.

11 Come back up through the same spot with the weaving wire and pull the wire tight. String the spacer bead and a 6° seed bead on the wire. Push the weaving wire through the spacer and the other side of the opened spot on the second section (**j**). Pull the weaving wire tight (be sure the seed bead sits straight).

String the weaving wire around and through the seed bead again for a stronger connection (**k**).

12 Repeat steps 9–11 to add four seed beads on each end. Work inward, until the two sides are completely connected.

TIP If you are having trouble getting your weaving wire through, make a path for the wire with the T-pin. I do this as often as needed, which seems to be a lot as the wires tighten up when more are added. It is worth it, though, for a strong and beautiful piece.

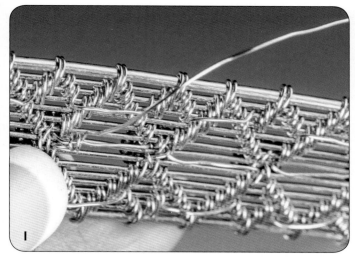

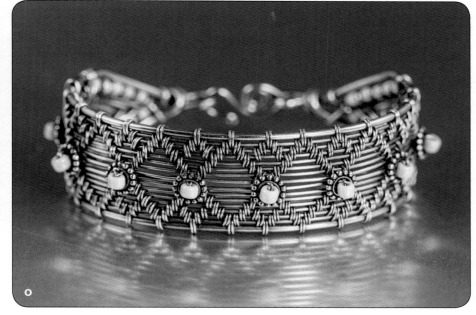

13 When you have added four seed beads from each end and they meet in the middle, wrap the wire ends together twice on the back side **(l)**. Trim the wire close and pinch it down. Do this with the other weaving wire and pinch it down.

14 Complete each end with the Crisscross Finishing Technique (p. 24). Make Double-Wrapped Loops (p. 21) on each end **(m)**.

15 Mold the bracelet to fit your wrist.

16 Make a Gooseneck Hook (p. 20) and slide it on one of the Double-Wrapped Loops **(n)**.

17 Create a finish with liver of sulfur (p. 25) **(o)**. Hand buff with a polishing cloth.

Twist and Turn
Woven Bracelet

This project is unusual. As the name implies, there is a twist involved with this piece. Begin weaving in one direction and then do a 90-degree turn and weave in a new direction for a unique wired center for the focal area of the piece. This is a challenging piece that will hone your wire skills. I am confident you can push yourself and achieve anything you set your mind on.

Materials

- 6½ ft. 20-gauge dead-soft copper wire
- 9 ft. 24-gauge dead-soft copper wire
- 21 in. 16-gauge dead-soft square copper wire
- **20** 8º seed beads

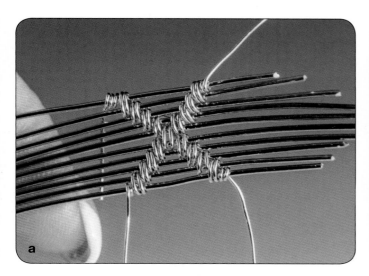

Complete the intersection of both sides. On the bottom section, work Downhill Flame Stitch Weave, Double-Wrap (p. 18) to base wire #1. On the top section, use the top weaving wire to complete the Uphill Flame Stitch Weave, Double Wrap (p. 17) to base wire #10. Leave the weaving wires as they are and do not trim them (a). They will be used later to add on beads and turtleneck them.

5 Crisscross the base wires on the right side of the weave. Make the bend 90 degrees from the start (b).

6 Crisscross the left side (c). Try to keep the base wires as lined up and straight as you can.

1 Cut 10 7½-in. pieces of 20-gauge wire for the base wires. Cut two 18-in. pieces of 24-gauge wire for the weaving wires for the center section and for turtlenecking the seed beads in the central part of the bracelet.

2 Work the Uphill Wire Preparation, Double Wrap (p. 14) on five 20-gauge base wires. These will be the bottom section base wires #1–#5. Set aside.

3 Complete the Downhill Wire Preparation, Double Wrap (p. 15) on five 20-gauge wires. These will be the top section base wires #6–#10.

4 Pick up both sections and place the downhill prep work on top.

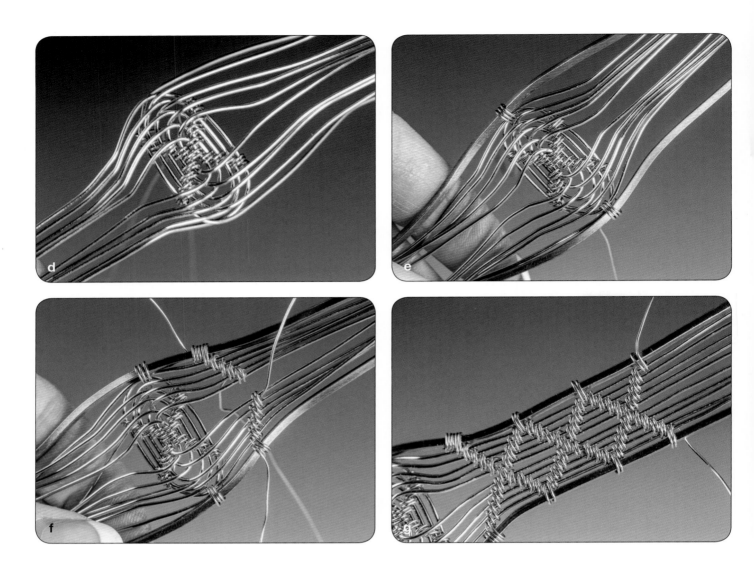

7 Bring the base wires inward so they start to line up to the other group. This is the tricky part—to get the base wires to curve slightly so they meet up with the other side in the middle and stay straight in line. Do this on both sides (**d**).

8 Pick up two 11-in. 16-gauge wires and make a gentle curve in the center. These wires will frame the woven section and provide strength for the bracelet. Once they are slightly curved, place one on the outside of the woven section. Using the long end of one of the weaving wires, push it through the spot where the two outside base wires crossed each other, and bind the outside base wires to the 16-gauge framing wire by wrapping the weaving wire around it three times. Leave the weaving wire there—do not trim. Repeat on the other side. The extra weaving wire will be used later to add on two beads and turtleneck them (**e**).

9 Cut two 3-ft. pieces of 24-gauge wire for the weaving wires for the right side. Start at the top framing wire, wrap it twice with the end of one of the weaving wires and complete the Downhill Wire Preparation, Double Wrap (p. 14) for the top six base wires. On the bottom section, pick up a 3-ft. piece of 24-gauge weaving wire and complete the Uphill Wire Preparation, Double Wrap (p. 14) (**f**).

10 Connect the top and bottom weave patterns (p. 18). Weave 2½ hills of the Flame Stitch Weave, Double Wrap (alternating uphill and downhill pattern) (p. 17, 18) (**g**). Stop there and do not trim the weaving wires.

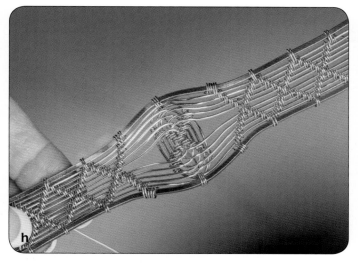

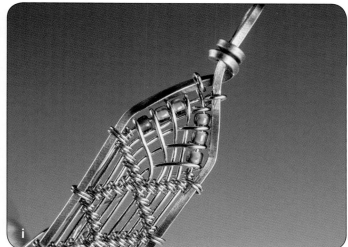

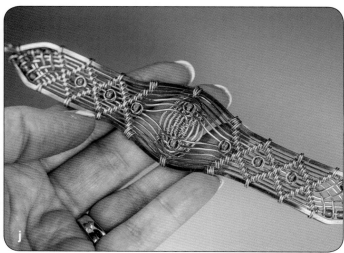

11 Repeat steps 6 and 7 for the other side **(h)**. Notice how the weave gives the base wires their spacing and keeps them in line? I love that.

12 Complete the Crisscross Finished End (p. 24), adding 8° seed beads between the crisscross wires on each side **(i)**. Do this on each end.

13 I placed the seed beads in the center of each of the diamonds in the pattern and gave them a Turtleneck for strength (p. 19), but you can place your seed beads anywhere you like. Using one of the weaving wires on the right, I came in from behind, added three seed beads, and Turtlenecked each one. From the left side, I did the same with one of the remaining weaving wires from that side. Trim the weaving wires that are not in use and tie off the ones that added on the seed beads **(j)**.

14 Make a Gooseneck Hook (p. 20) out of 16-gauge square wire for the clasp and attach it to the end, inside one of the loops of the bracelet.

15 Curve the bracelet to the contour of your wrist.

16 Create a finish with liver of sulfur (p. 25) **(k)** and hand buff.

Double-Crossed
Woven
Bracelet

This stunning bracelet has a large center focal bead. The weaving technique is nearly the same as the Scalloped Edge Bracelet (p. 58), only with a few more base wires, and an added stone and bezel. The woven bezel has two open ends, which make it a bit tricky, but with practice, you can get it. A few seed beads placed throughout bring continuity of color and visual interest.

Materials
- 19 in. 14-gauge dead-soft copper wire
- 7 ft. 20-gauge dead-soft copper wire
- 8 ft. 24-gauge dead-soft copper wire
- 20x25mm cabochon
- **18** 8º seed beads

Materials for the Bezel:
- 3 ft. 20-gauge dead-soft copper wire
- 2 ft. 24-gauge dead-soft copper wire

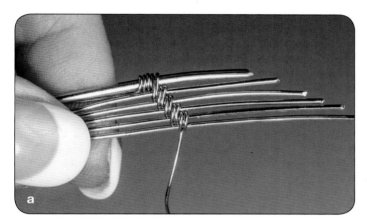

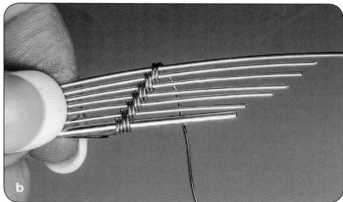

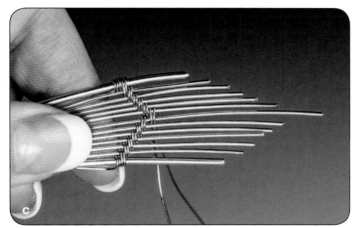

1 Cut two 9½-in. pieces of 14-gauge wire for the outer frame wires. Cut 11 7½-in. pieces of 20-gauge wire for the base wires. Cut two 3½-ft. pieces of 24-gauge wire for the weaving wires.

2 Pick up a 14-gauge base wire and wrap the end of a weaving wire around it three times. Complete the Downhill Wire Preparation, Double Wrap (p. 15) for six base wires (**a**). Set aside.

3 Pick up a new 14-gauge base wire, wrap a weaving wire around three times, and complete the Uphill Wire Preparation, Double Wrap (p. 14) for seven base wires (**b**).

4 Place the first section above the second section. Using the top weaving wire, wrap twice around base wires #7 and #8 (**c**). This unites the

two sections as we begin the snake weave.

5 Starting with the bottom weaving wire, wrap twice around base wires #6 and #7. Base wire #7 is the center wire and also the shared wire for this next part. Work Double Snake Weave (p. 12) for eight stitches (**d**).

TIP To make it easier to identify the center wire, pull it out a little farther than all the other base wires (see photo c). This will help you as you work the Snake Weave.

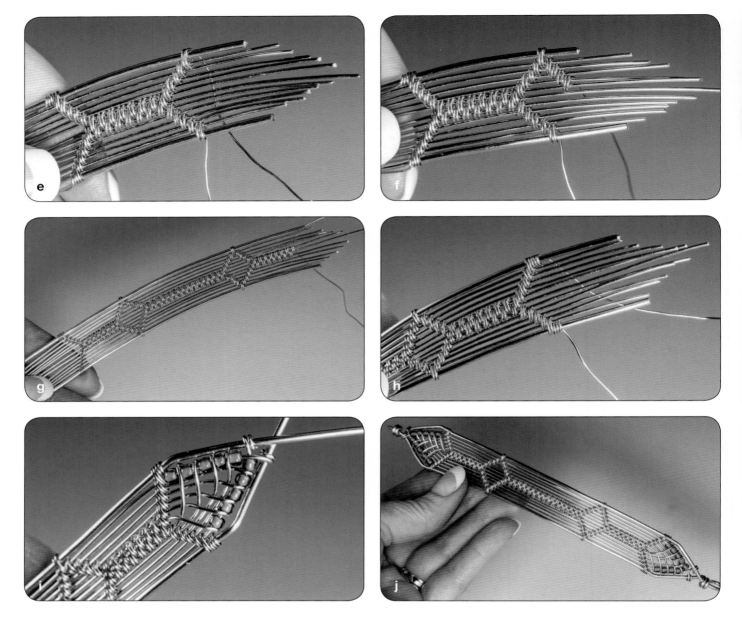

NOTE *The weave will separate and create diamond shapes.*

6 Bring the top weaving wire between base wires #7 and #8. Work Uphill Flame Stitch Weave, Double Wrap (p. 17) to the top of the hill. On the lower section, jump the bottom weaving wire down from behind and come up between base wires #4 and #5. Wrap twice around base wires #5 and #6. Work Downhill Flame Stitch Weave, Double Wrap (p. 18) to the bottom of the hill (**e**).

7 On the upper half, work four stitches of Downhill Flame Stitch, Double Wrap (**f**).

8 On the lower half, work Uphill Flame Stitch, Double Wrap to the middle to include wrapping base wires #6 and #7 twice. Just as you did when you were joining the two sections together before, bring the top weaving wire down to wrap base wires #7 and #8 twice. Complete the Double Snake Weave for 16 stitches. This makes the foundation for the focal stone. Separate the weave as you did in step 6. Create the same diamond shape in the weave. When the two weaving wires come back together, work Double Snake Weave for eight stitches (**g**).

9 Repeat step 6 to separate the weave on both the upper and lower sections. Wrap the upper weaving wire around base wire #13 three times (**h**). Trim each weaving wire close on the back and pinch it down.

10 Center the weave on the base wires and complete a Crisscross Finished End (p. 24) on each end of the bracelet, but start with one seed bead on base wire #12 to make up for the odd number of base wires (**i**).

11 Form a Double-Wrapped Loop (p. 21) on the ends of the crisscross sections (**j**). This part of the piece is finished.

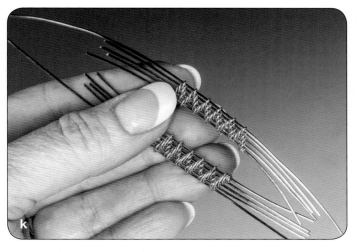

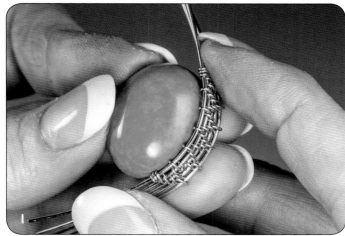

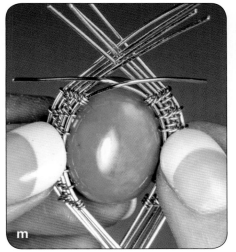

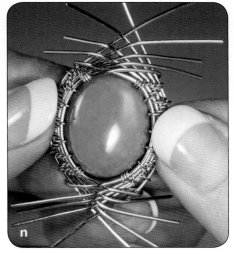

12 Now we'll begin the double crossed bezel. Cut two 6-in. pieces of 20-gauge wire for the outside base wires. Cut eight 3-in. pieces of 20-gauge wire for the remaining base wires. Cut two 12-in. pieces of 24-gauge weaving wire.

13 Weave the bezel sides: Complete an Uphill Wire Preparation, Single Wrap (**p. 13**) with a 24-gauge weaving wire, four 3-in. pieces and one 6-in. piece. Work six hills total of Flame Stitch Weave, Single Wrap (**p. 16**). Once completed, repeat to make an identical piece. Turn it 180 degrees so that it is a mirror image of the first bezel side (**k**).

14 Using the stone to help mold the shape, push both pieces of the bezel onto the side of the stone (**l**).

15 Crisscross the base wires of each side of the bezel. Pull the first two base wires down and over the opposite side so that they almost touch the woven part (**m**). This indicates where you should make the first loops on the crossed wires. Turn it around and do the same thing on the other side—crisscross the wires and pull the first two down.

16 This is important: You must stabilize the open ends so you can make a true fitting. Do this by wrapping the first two base wires on each side around the opposite side with a loose loop (**n**). It should not be tightened yet, just wrapped around the edges to hold the bezel in place so you can fit the other base wires.

17 With the first two base wires holding the shape, wrap the other base wires around the opposite sides, trim them about ⅜ in., and make a loose loop around the outside base wire (**o**). Try not to pull in on the outside base wire and keep the original shape established by the first two base wires.

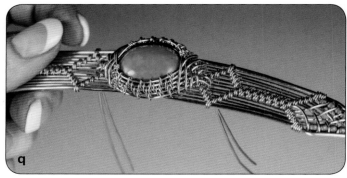

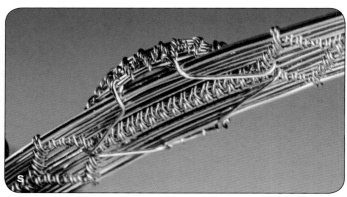

18 Wrap the ends of the other side as you did the first, taking care to maintain the shape of the bezel. On the back, tighten the loops by trimming them if they are too long and pinching them down. Keep checking the fit by putting the stone back in and molding the wire to the contour (**p**).

19 Bend the two long base wires on either side of the bezel straight back at a 45-degree angle. Slide the two base wires inside the diamond pattern with the center wire between them. Do this on both sides. Use a T-pin to make room for the base wires if they don't want to go in there. Put the stone in the bezel and slide it up to the bracelet to secure it (**q**).

20 On the back, bend the base wires to the side, go through base wire #5 of the bezel, and pull it straight down. Don't tighten it yet; leave it a little loose. Do this to all four base wires so they hold the bezel right up against the bracelet (**r**).

21 As you make the loops, check to make sure the bezel is in the center of the bracelet. Tighten the loops underneath when you are sure the bezel is placed where you want it. Trim the loops and pinch them down to tighten. Trim the base wires and pinch them down (**s**).

Finishing

22 Make a Gooseneck Hook (p. 20) and attach it to the end of the bracelet. Bend the bracelet to fit your wrist and try it on.

23 Create a finish with liver of sulfur (p. 25) and hand buff.

NOTE Adding embellishments is always the fun part for me. I chose to place four seed beads right at the points of separation of the weave to emphasize the diamond shapes. I added the beads and Turtlenecked (p. 19) them. They add the finishing touch that makes the project shine. It usually doesn't take much—just a few beads at the right places.

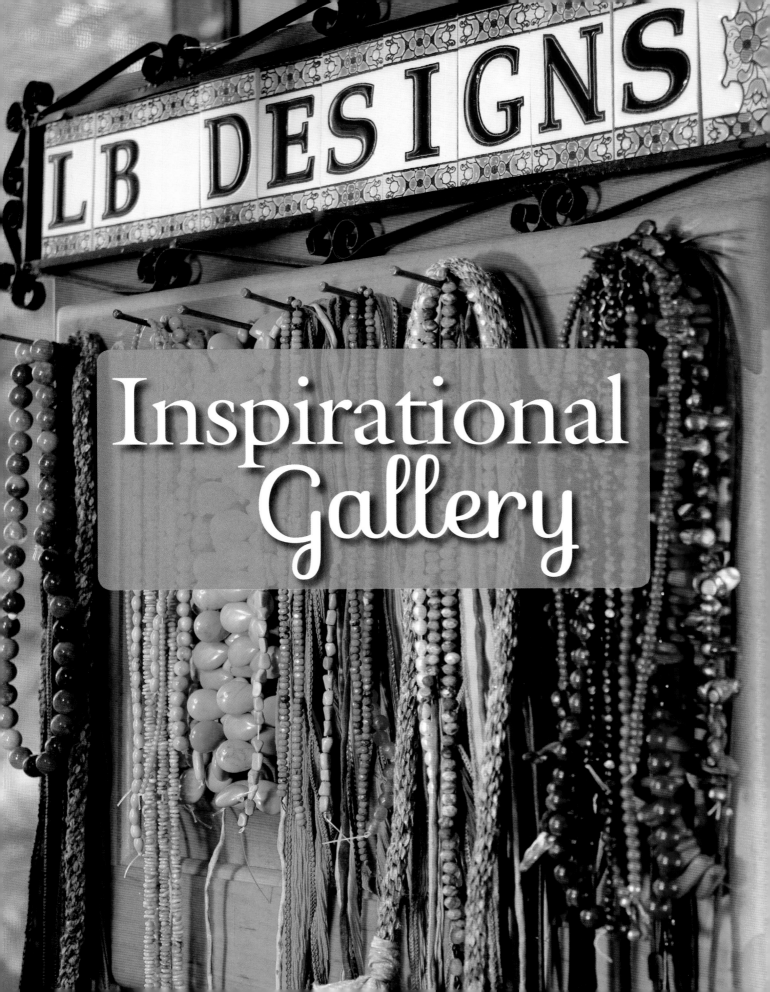

LB DESIGNS

Inspirational
Gallery

1

3

2

It is my hope that you explore the wonderful world of wire weaving by trying as many variations as you can dream up. These weaving techniques are remarkably versatile and marvelously fun to play with. Here are just a few of the variations I have done. I hope they help inspire you to be creative with these techniques and enjoy your own designs.

1 How wide can you go? This bracelet has 20 base wires to make it the widest bracelet I have done so far. Maybe you can go even wider! Making a wide bracelet gives you lots of room to embellish. Here I added amethyst and seed beads to give it lots of personality.

2 This sterling and fine-silver bracelet has a sleeping beauty turquoise centerpiece I made with metal clay, but you can add any centerpiece with holes drilled

on either side. I wired the piece on to the bracelet after it was woven to fit the centerpiece. I used a filigree link to give the back some pizazz as I wired the centerpiece on. I also used chain and a toggle for a clasp.

3 This locket is made with two woven bezels of single Flame Stitch that frame a domed copper disk in each side. I modified the bail to make a hinge and added a latch as the piece was

woven. On the inside, I made a little coil as I stitched the disk to the woven bezel to help hide the holes I drilled in the copper disks.

4 Here's a bit of a variation for the Twist and Turn Woven Bracelet (p. 82): As I made the twist and crossed the wires, I placed a sugilite cabochon to be captured by the crossing wires. Adding more purple seed beads in the mix emphasizes the color of the stone.

5 Fringe will jazz up an otherwise plain woven bezel pendant. This varisite cabochon has a horizontally woven bezel. While I was weaving along the bottom, I placed links of a chain to add the fringe at every transition from downhill to uphill in the weaving pattern.

6 This pendant has a plain woven frame of Snake Weave. I added three layers of embellishment dangled in the middle and stitched a Russian spiral necklace to give

it plenty of contrasting texture. Is there a limit to embellishment? Let's keep pushing the envelope.

7 To create a different look from a woven bezel, I placed this labradorite pendant upside down and added a dangle at the bottom. Any pear-shaped stone will do this nicely. The back has a hidden double bail for variety and a little fun.

8 This necklace is similar in construction to the Scalloped Edge Woven Bracelet (p. 58)—it's just made in smaller sections and curved to fit at the neckline. Double-Wrapped Loops capture a turquoise bead to link the three sections together. There are many varieties of bracelet techniques you have learned that can be used in smaller proportion for links in necklaces. Try to think out of the box and I know you'll come up with many wonderful new designs.

9 For a different point of view, this cabochon is woven vertically instead of horizontally. It is a bit more challenging to center it, but well worth it when it's done. Any shaped cab can be the main focal element in your bracelet design.

10 The Double-Crossed Woven Bracelet (p. 86) elements are used in this necklace. The woven bezel section are the links instead of the center focal.

11 Here is a variation of the Crisscross Technique used for finishing bracelet ends. This wrap begins at the bottom with six wires bound together: four crisscross on the front, one goes up the side, and one goes up the back. They reunite at the bail. Add the fringe after the wrap is done.

12 Adding seed beads into the weave is an effective way to give color and texture to a design. The little wire swirls and the Tila beads were "stitched" on after the weaving.

About the Author

Lisa Barth is a wire jewelry artist, a senior-level certified Metal Clay instructor, and a professional jewelry photographer from Atlanta, Georgia. She actively teaches from her studio, around the country, and internationally to share her unique techniques of design in metal clay and wirework with others. Lisa also teaches jewelry photography and has had her photos published in several magazines.

In addition to teaching, Lisa has written articles for several magazines, including the cover of *Bead&Button*, *Australian Beading*, *Bead Style*, and *Metal Clay Artist*, and books including several volumes of *Creative Beading*.

Her first book, *Designing from the Stone*, is sold on Amazon.com. Bezel setting stones is her specialty, and Lisa enjoys sharing her expertise in designing organically, achieving harmony between the stone and the setting. She is always learning and pushing herself to achieve excellence as she endeavors to share her God-given passion for creativity. **Col 3:23** *Whatever you do, work at it wholeheartedly as though you were doing it for the Lord and not merely for people.*

Much thanks to Maryann Sieler (Stones That Rock, www.cabochon.ws.) for her beautifully cut stones.

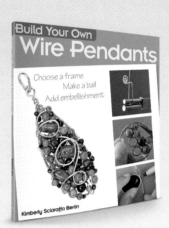